Freedom and Discipline

Introductory Studies in Philosophy of Education
Series Editors: PHILIP SNELDERS and COLIN WRINGE

Freedom and Discipline

RICHARD SMITH

Lecturer in Education, University of Durham

GEORGE ALLEN & UNWIN

Boston   Sydney

© Richard Smith, 1985.
This book is copyright under the Berne Convention.
No reproduction without permission. All rights reserved.

George Allen & Unwin (Publishers) Ltd,
40 Museum Street, London WC1A 1LU, UK

George Allen & Unwin (Publishers) Ltd,
Park Lane, Hemel Hempstead, Herts HP2 4TE, UK

Allen & Unwin, Inc.,
Fifty Cross Street, Winchester, Mass. 01890, USA

George Allen & Unwin Australia Pty Ltd,
8 Napier Street, North Sydney, NSW 2060, Australia

First published in 1985.

British Library Cataloguing in Publication Data

Smith, Richard
    Freedom and discipline. – (Introductory studies in philo-
sophy of education)
1. School discipline – Philosophy
I. Title   II. Series
371.5'01   LB3012
ISBN 0–04–370158–2
ISBN 0–04–370159–0 Pbk

Library of Congress Cataloging in Publication Data

Smith, Richard (Richard D.)
    Freedom and discipline.
(Introductory studies in philosophy of education)
Bibliography: p.
Includes index.
1. School discipline – Philosophy. 2. Rewards and
punishments in education. 3. Classroom management.
I. Title. II. Series.
LB3012.S67   1985   371.5   84–24287
ISBN 0–04–370158–2
ISBN 0–04–370159–0 Pbk

Set in 10 on 11 point Plantin by Phoenix Photosetting, Chatham
and printed in Great Britain by Biddles Ltd, Guildford, Surrey

371.5
S65

86-1175

Contents

for Henry and Sam

glad and free

Editors' Foreword

Books that are available to students of philosophy of education may, in general, be divided into two types. There are collections of essays and articles making up a more or less random selection; and there are books which explore a single theme or argument in depth but, having been written to break new ground, are often unsuitable for general readers or those near the beginning of their course. The Introductory Studies in Philosophy of Education are intended to fill what is widely regarded as an important gap in this range.

The series aims to provide a collection of short, readable works which, besides being philosophically sound, will seem relevant and accessible to future and existing teachers without a previous knowledge of philosophy or of philosophy of education. In the planning of the series, account has necessarily been taken of the tendency of present-day courses of teacher education to follow a more integrated and less discipline-based pattern than formerly. Account has also been taken of the fact that students on three- and four-year courses, as well as those on shorter postgraduate and in-service courses, quite understandably expect their theoretical studies to have a clear bearing on their practical concerns, and on their dealings with children. Each book, therefore, starts from a real and widely recognized problem in the educational field, and explores the main philosophical approaches which illuminate and clarify it or suggest a coherent standpoint even when they do not claim to provide a solution. Account is taken of the work of both mainstream philosophers and philosophers of education. For students who wish to pursue particular questions in depth, each book contains a bibliographical essay or a substantial list of suggestions for further reading. It is intended that a full range of the main topics recently discussed by philosophers of education should eventually be covered by the series.

Besides having considerable experience in the teaching of philosophy of education, the majority of the authors writing in the series have already received some recognition in their particular fields. In addition, therefore, to reviewing and criticizing existing work, each author has his or her own positive contribution to make to further discussion.

Questions of discipline and order arise wherever formal education is practised, and are particularly acute for those training to teach or in their first school posts. Recent writing on education and schooling has tended to depict teaching as the deployment of 'skills' and competent teachers as those who successfully 'manage' their classes. This approach is criticized in this book as manipulative and destructive of the kind of pupil–teacher relationship conducive to any but the most trivial kind of learning.

Thus the philosophical issues which Richard Smith explores are shown to have their roots in problems associated with current thinking and practice. The author's positive theses also have considerable practical relevance. He argues for a thorough reappraisal of the nature and basis of the teacher's authority and demonstrates the importance of a proper understanding of the function of punishment. He suggests that many of the problems of discipline teachers meet may actually stem from inappropriate ways of treating pupils, and shows that solutions to these problems must be compatible with the degree of initiative and personal responsibility that it is the business of education to foster.

Philip Snelders
Colin Wringe

Preface

This is an introductory text: I would like to think that amongst other things it introduced the reader to the fact that philosophy matters, to education and schooling as to all activities in our world. Thus although I have tried to do justice to the main philosophical approaches to my subject I have devoted most space to arguing for what I believe is true, and not been sorry if a degree of feeling here and there could not quite be excluded.

But for my students in the Durham University School of Education there would have been little feeling and probably no book. It would be unfair to single out anybody by name. They will find echoes here of our dialectic and know how much I have learned from them.

I am also grateful to Geof Alred, who reassured me that Chapter 9 would pass; to Bob Graham, for reading and commenting on all the manuscript, for endless discussion and support; and to my wife Jenny for her patience despite being about to produce in an altogether more impressive way.

1

The Disrupted Teacher

The practical problems which face all teachers, and especially those in training and in their early years in the profession, are the subject of this book. At the same time it is written from a philosophical point of view. People often think that the practical and the philosophical are at opposite poles. Nothing could be more mistaken. Thinking clearly about what you are doing, which is the heart of philosophy, is a highly practical activity because it can transform practice, often out of all recognition. It is easy to illustrate this from any area of everyday life. Consider the mother in a supermarket with a fractious toddler pulling tins off the shelves and throwing a tantrum because he wants sweets. What exactly does the child's behaviour amount to? One mother might say 'He's playing me up'; another might explain that this is attention-seeking behaviour, due to his father's recent absence from home and the child's resulting sense of insecurity. The descriptions are not wholly exclusive of each other, for clearly a child may 'play up' precisely in order to seek attention. But the way we conceive of the child's behaviour here and the language we use to describe it, to others or ourselves, goes a long way towards determining how we treat it. The first description suggests a good slap, while the second suggests sympathy and reassurance. This is of course to say nothing about which description and treatment is more accurate and appropriate. The second mother might be unduly influenced by fashionable, pseudo-psychological jargon.

To take a second example, we are not usually pleased at finding a shop assistant surly and unhelpful. But again this depends on our perspective, the way that we conceive of his behaviour. If we see working from nine until five every day as wage-slavery which is bound to induce a sense of alienation then we can take our encounter with the unhelpful shop assistant as one more reassuring piece of evidence that our thesis is satisfactory. Thus Howard Kirk, hero of Malcolm Bradbury's novel *The History Man*, regards the world:

The assistant looks at him; he is young, with a beard, and wears a maroon jacket with a yellow Smile badge on the lapel; this leaves his face free to be very surly. Howard sees with gratification the indignation of the employed and oppressed, the token resistance.

All of this applies with great force to the problems of teachers: it makes a great deal of difference just how you conceive of the problems you have, what perspectives you view events from. Imagine, for example, the teacher faced with a class of thirty children to whom he is to teach geography or history or English. They ignore his arrival in the classroom, except for a few ironic calls of greeting; they continue shouting and fighting, running about the room, utterly hostile to his efforts to impose some order and begin the lesson. In a short time he is reduced to despair. Now there is clearly a problem here. But what exactly is it? Four people might see it in four very different ways, from four different perspectives.

One teacher might think of this as essentially a question of effective teaching and learning: of learning that is not taking place because he is not doing his job of teaching. From this perspective the solution that suggests itself is simply that of teaching the material better. Trainee teachers often seem to think in these terms. Perhaps much of the responsibility lies with those who convey the impression that the answer to all teaching difficulties lies in making lessons interesting enough, as I once heard it put, to distract a kamikaze pilot. Our first teacher accordingly brings wall-charts, posters and slides. He concentrates on the more lurid episodes of history or features of the children's own environment or he tries to read them poems about football or adolescent sexuality, in the hope of catching their interest for long enough for them to settle down and become absorbed in the lesson.

A second teacher might think of the problem as one of authority and insubordination. He is the teacher in that classroom, he feels, and the children are supposed to do as he tells them. That is what teachers are for. Accordingly he tries to establish his authority, first with threats of punishment and then attempts at punishment. He wants to reduce the class to a state of orderly preparedness before he starts, and his fundamental attitude is that they should be orderly just because they ought – because that's what schools are all about. I once knew a teacher of considerable experience whose every class was chaotic and rowdy. He held the view that to try to impose some order by better organization or by improving the way he taught his subject was a kind of abdication of the teacher's role, a specious and dishonest way of achieving what he wanted. The children were to obey because he was the figure of authority: nothing else would do. There are problems here of a manifestly theoretical or philosophical nature: what do we mean by 'authority'? What gives a teacher any *right* to punish pupils? I shall return to these particular issues later. At this stage it is important to appreciate what the practical effects may be of conceiving teaching problems vaguely in terms of authority. For example, teachers are often advised to 'cultivate an air of authority'. This is unfortunately not easy to distinguish from an authoritarian manner which verges on something like bullying, a manner probably destructive of any pleasure the teacher might take in his work and any respect children might feel for him. Then again some young teachers, thinking similarly in terms of authority, conclude that the first requirement of a teacher is a kind of natural authority or charisma, and that if they do not have such a quality they are defeated from the beginning.

A third way of conceiving the classroom problem I outlined above is in terms of control and order. There is a straightforward sense in which we can hardly fail to think of it like this: the children are obviously disorderly and the teacher cannot control them. But it puts the business in a very different light if you see your task as introducing order, rather than imposing authority, as controlling the children's behaviour rather more in the manner of a traffic-policeman than a sergeant-major. If you see the problem in this light you might turn to the kinds of strategies that are described in manuals of classroom management, such as Michael Marland's *The Craft of the Classroom* (Marland, 1980). The comparison with a traffic-policeman is apt, for such guides to classroom survival often lay considerable emphasis on matters like organizing the flow of pupils into and around the classroom, establishing where they are to sit and procedures for moving around, asking questions and so on. The stress is on order rather than authority, on defining the situation in which teaching is to take place as a preliminary to the teaching itself. Although there is a danger here of merely manipulating children (a matter to which I shall return), entirely comparable with the dangers of bullying them, it is comforting to conceive the problem as one of order and control in this way: it takes a lot of the heat out of the situation. To see the pupils as confused and undirected rather than as rowdy and disobedient is to feel less threatened and (the importance of perspective again) it is also to perceive the problem as one you can learn to do something about. Perhaps, this perspective suggests, you do not need charisma to sort out the tangles of the classroom any more than the traffic-policeman does to keep the traffic moving smoothly: in both cases there are quite simple techniques which can be learned.

A fourth teacher might view the problem here from a perspective similar to Howard Kirk's. If he regarded 'deviance' simply as a label which those in authority attach to various social and economic groups they disapprove of, and if he believed such groups are bound to resent such labelling and act so as to fulfil its prophecy, he might welcome the rebellious behaviour of some of his classes, seeing it as the natural outcome of an unjust system and as likely to lead to the overthrow of the system in the end. There certainly are many teachers who regard, say, the label 'remedial', applied to a pupil, as more informative about the attitudes of the school's hierarchy than about the individual child, and who see such children as the victims of a very raw deal and their reactions to the way they are treated as entirely understandable. This perspective implies a very different approach to these pupils' disorderly behaviour in the classroom, starting from sympathy with their difficulties rather than simple condemnation.

These, then, are the kinds of problems, and the kinds of perspective on the problems, which I shall be dealing with in this book. I shall at every stage be drawing attention to the importance of thinking carefully about the various terms – language, concepts and ideas – that we use to contemplate the problems and discuss them with one another. Such terms are the elements from which different perspectives are formed, and it may turn out that some terms, and the perspectives built from them, can be shown to be confused or ambiguous. It is these confusions and ambiguities that we have to explore and unravel, for until our conception of the problem makes sense our attempts to solve it are hopeless. Sometimes we may find that in the process of clarification the substantial problem effectively disappears. Bringing one's thinking into good order is neither a luxury nor an optional extra. A person whose thinking is confused, whose perspective is distorted or narrow, is being disrupted just as much as somebody whose activities are being reduced to chaos by more obvious and tangible disruptions, of the sort that a class of lively children can engineer. Good practice requires clear and well-ordered thinking, rather than the muddled self-contradictions we are all prone to that waste so much of our energy. I supply an example of this from my own experience. When I started teaching I felt obliged to take in and mark all my classes' exercise books religiously. That is, I collected them about twice a week and indicated every mistake of spelling and punctuation, as well as errors of content. I think I must have felt that teachers must not overlook mistakes. After a year or so, however, I began to realize that this was largely a waste of time. The amount of red ink I was covering

4

exercises with was in itself discouraging for pupils. It made it harder for them to spot which were the bad or important mistakes, and in any case I was tending to imagine that my job as a marker of books ended when I gave the books back: I wasn't ensuring, for example, that correct spellings were copied out. So instead I began to concentrate on correcting only certain sorts of mistakes in each exercise (it might be particular spellings one week, the use of the comma the next), and then I would make sure the corrections were noted. I could also devote parts of lessons to the same business. Of course I had to make it clear to the children (and sometimes to their parents too) that this was what I was doing, so that they did not think that absence of red ink meant all their spellings were correct. At any rate the effect of all this was that the children did seem to improve a little faster than before, and I certainly did not have to spend nearly so much time over my piles of marking. I think, looking back, that I had felt obliged to mark conscientiously but I had given no proper thought at all to what 'marking their books' might involve.

The business of sorting out muddled thinking can fairly be called 'philosophical', for philosophers have nearly always seen one of their main jobs as clearing away confusion. Not surprisingly philosophy, like many other activities, can become highly technical and inaccessible to those without special training, but there is a sense in which we are always thinking philosophically when we try to get clear about the logic of our thinking and the terminology that we use: when we do something as ordinary as wondering whether it really makes much sense to dignify a badly thought-out mish-mash of a curriculum with the adjective 'integrated', for example, or whether it really follows from the fact that a child comes from a very deprived background that he has no choice in what he does and so cannot be held responsible for his actions. I have some sympathy with people who think issues like these are the province of common sense rather than of any academic specialism. But common sense can be refined and improved, even in the most sensible person, to the point where it becomes something rather uncommon. And this is perhaps the point where it becomes very hard to distinguish from philosophy. The following extract from Plato's *Republic* illustrates this well. There is no technical language here, yet the manner in which Plato represents Socrates as refuting Thrasymachus is more thorough and devastating than most of us manage against our opponents in argument. Thrasymachus has been claiming that wrongdoing is a powerful weapon and a source of strength to the wrongdoer, for he is unhindered in his pursuit of his objectives by considerations of right and wrong:

5

Socrates:	Tell me if you suppose that any group of people, whether it is a state or an army or a crowd of criminals or thieves, can manage to carry out any kind of wrongdoing together if they do wrong to each other.
Thrasymachus:	No.
Soc.:	They are more likely to be successful if they do not wrong each other?
Thras.:	Yes, they are.
Soc.:	Of course. And the reason is that if they wrong each other that will cause hatred and disunity to break out among them, while if they deal fairly with each other they will enjoy common objectives and friendly relations with each other . . . It is the same with any two individuals. Wrongdoing will lead to them quarrelling and hating each other. They will be enemies to each other and to good men as well.
Thras.:	They will.
Soc.:	So what happens when there is wrongdoing in a state or a family or an army or any other organization is that it is made incapable of any shared enterprise because of disagreements and quarrels. It ends up at odds with itself, with its opponents and with all good men.
Thras.:	Yes, that is right.
Soc.:	Inevitably it has the same effects on the individual. Wrongdoing renders him ineffectual through internal conflicts and fragmentation of his objectives. It sets him at odds with himself and with all good men.

(*Republic*, 351C ff.)

The extract shows how at the dawn of philosophy the philosopher's business was seen as trying to bring some clear thinking to bear on complex issues where we quickly become muddled, such as the problem Thrasymachus raises here: how acting morally is a good for the moral agent as well as those he acts towards.

There are two other important points to make in connection with this passage from Plato. First, Plato's argument can hardly be quite right as it stands. He claims that the immoral man is rendered ineffectual by internal divisions or conflicts. Yet it is not hard to think of people, from history or one's own acquaintance, who are only too effectively unscrupulous or dishonest. My point here is that if we are ourselves thinking philosophically we must treat what philosophers say critically and not as if their words came engraved on tablets of stone. Secondly, although Plato's argument above may be flawed I think it contains the germ of a telling point about the nature of philosophy. Perhaps internal conflicts cause, not dramatic cases of wrongdoing and criminality, but more humdrum human failings and deficiencies. For example, the individual who is torn between the repudiation of 'middle-class' or 'bourgeois' values and the desire for security and expensive possessions is likely to find himself trapped in all sorts of minor pretences and evasions, in addition to his failure to discover a life-style he can commit himself to wholeheartedly. When we are thus divided against ourselves we risk pulling others into our muddle, misleading them about our loyalties and commitments. This is where internal conflict has those repercussions on the moral life that Plato made perhaps rather too much of. At any rate, being pulled in opposite directions is again often the result of failure to think properly about what one is doing. To take another example, close to the central concerns of this book, I often find trainee teachers are reluctant to impose order on a class of children, feeling (usually rather vaguely) that they have no right to constrain children's freedom. Michael Marland (1980) draws attention to the same phenomenon. At the same time they soon discover that if it is left in a state of supposed freedom a class can become so unruly that no pupil is free to do anything but contribute to the rowdiness. Unless the teacher gets his ideas sorted out here the urge to stop the chaos on the one hand and the anxiety on the other of unjustifiably imposing constraints are likely to go on pulling in different directions, with disastrous results.

In a case of this sort nothing else will do but to get clearer in one's mind about the notion of freedom (as I shall try to in Chapter 10) in order to see just what position one really wants to take up. The confused teacher must either find some way of justifying the free-for-all into which his lessons descend, or consider some variation on the familiar view that freedom is possible only within a framework of established limitations. Thinking through these issues is likely to be difficult and possibly uncomfortable, because some of a person's existing beliefs have to be abandoned or heavily modified if the contradiction among them is to be resolved. Giving up cherished beliefs is never easy, but the reward is the chance of becoming an individual who has achieved a measure of harmony among his beliefs and engagements and who as a result is surer and more confident in his actions.

One way of expressing the claims about philosophy that I have been making is to say that in the examination of one's beliefs and the language in which they are couched – in doing philosophy, that is –

7

there lies the possibility of a kind of freedom. It is the freedom from muddle and internal conflict or disruption. There may be beliefs we hold and other items in our consciousness which are just a drag on us. Perhaps they became so to speak part of the furniture of our minds before we were in a position to make our own decisions about these matters: sometimes we can trace our ideas directly back to parents, teachers or other powerful influences. However we can assess the contents of our consciousnesses and decide which of such items we want to keep and which to reject. There can often be a remarkable sense of liberation in deciding that something one had always felt obliged (perhaps rather unhappily) to maintain has no rational justification and can safely be jettisoned: that it is, perhaps, just a piece of lumber from the past, loaded on to one's childhood shoulders, that one is well rid of. I believe that the freedom which thinking philosophically thus confers is not just one freedom among many but is a central and highly significant kind of freedom. This is one reason why this book contains the word 'freedom' in its title. The other reason is that it is at the centre of the various issues I shall be discussing throughout the book. Questions of control, punishment and authority revolve around the notion of freedom – of what freedom is and who may impose constraints on it, for what reasons and on what conditions. Freedom is, so to speak, the central idea, the sun of this particular universe, and it exercises its gravitational pull and casts its warmth and light (which can occasionally be blinding) and its fascination on the satellite concepts.

Because talk of freedom will be at the heart of all I have to say in this book I shall conclude this introductory chapter with some discussion of the notion of freedom. It is important to do this here because anyone who is convinced, as many people seem to be, that human beings have no freedom at all, that they simply do whatever they have been conditioned to do, is likely to find portions of this book, containing as it does talk of choice and responsibility, rather puzzling. If we really are at the mercy of our environment, of what our parents, schooling and society have made of us, or if our genetic endowment has the effect of a programme fed into a computer, dictating the course of our life and making any sense of freedom an illusion, then it would be quite correct to find choice and responsibility puzzling notions, for they could have no place in discussions of human behaviour. This is one more reason why getting clear about freedom *matters*. Under total conditioning, without any freedom at all, there would be no sense in praising or blaming people for their actions, and it is not clear that there could be any objection to manipulating them into doing whatever the state or any other controlling agency required in the name of what was good for them.

It is, I believe, a mistake to discuss the problem here simply in terms of whether we have freedom or not, as if mankind were either completely free or entirely lacking in freedom, with no shades of grey allowable. In any case I am not at all sure what 'complete freedom' could be or whether it would be desirable to be in such a state. Rather our question should be just how much freedom, or what *sort* of freedom, we have: the two questions go together. It will be convenient to handle the issue in the form in which it often arises in everyday life and to consider how we are to reply to the person whom I shall call, for the sake of brevity, 'the determinist': the person who asserts that everything we do we do as a result of the environment we live in or the way we have been brought up or something of the sort, so that any sense of freedom we may have in our actions is illusory. There is more than one form of determinism and many who regard themselves as determinists would not put their case in this way. However the label will do for present purposes as long as it is understood that the whole subject of determinism could be treated much more subtly than I shall attempt here.

It will be easier to consider the strengths and weaknesses of the determinist's case with a particular context in mind. Let us take one of the everyday difficulties the teacher faces: what is sometimes called euphemistically 'the extraneous comment'. The teacher hands out a pile of exercise books which he took in to mark the previous week and begins to say, 'When I marked these books . . .', intending to continue with some comments about the sorts of qualities he was hoping to find in the work. But his sentence is completed for him from the back row: '. . . about six months ago'. Now we might normally think that there are various ways open to the teacher of responding to this challenge, and that he is free to choose among them the one most appropriate to the particular situation – to this pupil and this class. But this is precisely what our determinist may want to deny. I have been present at many discussions about the best way of dealing with incidents of this sort when someone has tried to terminate the proceedings by complaining, in tones of injured realism, that discussion is useless: the teacher's course of action is dictated by such factors as the way he was himself brought up by his parents and treated at school, the prevailing atmosphere in the staffroom of the school where he works, attitudes to punishment and discipline allegedly characteristic of 'society', and so on. Can any reply be made to this?

The first point to make is that we can agree with quite a lot of what the determinist says without having to deny that people are in the end responsible for what they do or that their deliberations over different courses of action and the reasons for and against them are important and effective, and not just rationalizations to justify courses of action which their conditioning has forced them to adopt anyway. For it may be that at so-called 'moments of choice' we are pretty well bound, being the persons we are, to decide the way we do: still, perhaps, we are responsible for being the persons we are. We have the power over time slowly to change ourselves, to alter our habits, our patterns of motive and desire, and it is in this that a kind of freedom lies. In any case when we say that a person is bound to do something we are often imputing a high degree of predictability rather than literal inevitability. 'Knowing him', we say, 'he's bound to be slaving away over his books tonight – the exam's only a week away'. That this is not a case of true inevitability is shown by the fact that the person we are talking about may overhear and spend the evening down the pub just to spite us. The predictability of many people in large areas of their lives may be less a sign of lack of freedom than of their having arrived at a settled pattern of motives and interests. Anyone who knows me at all well should be confident of the outcome if I have a choice between going out to a formal dinner-party and staying in to finish the novel I'm reading. My predictability here is not a sign that I am 'conditioned' to prefer one sort of activity to the other: it is a result of having a well-developed, long-standing interest in literature and, importantly, in having thought about and accepted the place that literature has among my priorities. Predictability in a person's actions may be less a mark of conditioning or lack of freedom than a sign that he has attained a kind of settled state: he has worked out where he stands, so that his inclinations and interests do not pull him now in one direction and now in another.

I accept, then, that our imaginary teacher, faced with the problem of the extraneous comment, may so regularly and predictably 'choose' one solution rather than others that observers (perhaps his pupils) are inclined to wonder whether there is any real choice involved for him at all. Perhaps he always tried to cap such witticisms with quips of his own ('Yes, it takes me that long to read your writing'); perhaps he believes in a tariff of punishments, so that a three-sided imposition for such an offence is quite automatic. Perhaps he generally copes with such relatively minor incidents by regarding them simply as an interruption to the smooth flow of the lesson, pointing out that this is no part of what is supposed to be going on and returning as quickly as possible to the material he is teaching. None of this is any evidence at all that he must be acting the way he does simply in response to some sort of pressure or influence outside him, such as the ethos of his staffroom. It may rather be the result of his having more or less explicitly decided that this is the sort of teacher he wants to be, or (which comes to something like the same thing) in his having got into the habit of making this kind of response to minor incidents of indiscipline because he senses that it is of a piece with being the kind of teacher he sees himself as.

The determinist who has his wits about him is unlikely to be satisfied with this answer, however. Our capacity gradually to modify our ways of looking at the world and acting on it, to alter our perceptions and conceptions and the patterns of behaviour that rest on them, is a capacity, the determinist may argue, that we possess in greater or lesser degree because of our environment or our upbringing or whatever. The way in which we are inclined to view the world is itself something we owe to a multitude of external factors. So our freedom is not to be located there.

I would not want to underestimate the role that our circumstances play in shaping our consciousnesses. No doubt class, race and so on all play a part in suggesting different outlooks on life. To refuse to recognize this would be to deny that sociology and history, for example, have any valuable insights to offer. To acquire these insights, however, is to begin to transform one's consciousness away from that of a mere product of external forces. Certainly circumstances may have a powerful formative influence, but we can play an active role in relation to them: we can understand them, and to an extent (for it may require considerable effort) determine how much we want to incorporate these influences as part of our mature personalities. A very simple case of this is regional accent. That, I take it, is undoubtedly the product of our environment and upbringing. But for many people there comes a stage when they realize how their speech sounds to those from a different part of the country. Awareness of one's accent brings with it the possibility of deliberately losing it to acquire 'BBC English' instead, or of determinedly retaining it as part of one's roots and identity, perhaps in the face of disapproval from those who find the accent foreign and unattractive.

If the determinist continues to insist that we owe our every action, belief and attitude to external factors then there are two replies that can be made, a short one and a rather longer one. The short reply is that if his thesis is true of all opinions and assertions then it must be true of his own: his claiming that all we do and say is caused by heredity or environment or whatever must itself be put down to some such factor as parental influence, premature potty-training or bourgeois upbringing.

I think this reply is devastating to the determinist's case as it is usually put. But, perhaps because it is so short, some people seem to think it is just a clever trick. The longer reply, though it is no more than an amplification of the short one, may have more persuasive power. The point of the short answer is that the determinist must be taken as meaning that the only account which is for a moment to be entertained of why we do and say the things we do runs in terms of external causes, any appeal to reasons being mere rationalization. That is why the determinist's own case falls to the same sweeping axe: it can, on his own claim, be considered only on the same terms and not with reference to any reasons he may adduce. Now the longer reply consists in drawing out the absurdity of not taking reasons seriously, which is what the determinist does not do. For suppose that I am explaining to my class why I think *Animal Farm* can be read as a political allegory, for example, or why iron filings fall into a certain pattern round a magnet. I give the pupils reasons, and no one (I hope) is inclined in cases like these to suppose that what, as an English specialist, I say about *Animal Farm*, or what I say as a physicist about iron filings, is to be seen simply as the result of some sort of conditioning. I give *reasons* for my analysis of the novel or my assertions about iron filings: I indicate features of the novel or other observable properties of magnets which *justify* me in what I say. To talk of *Animal Farm* as a political allegory is something that would not even make sense unless we had some idea of what sorts of features would count as evidence for calling it that, and were prepared to refer to them. Such features are what give terms like 'allegory' their meaning.

If this is true for novels and magnetic fields, why should it be any less true for The Case of the Extraneous Comment and other aspects of the teacher's work? Here too a teacher can point to observable features of the situation which justify him in perceiving it in one way rather than others and in adopting a particular solution. The way I respond to the interruption from the back of the class really should depend on what I know about the class as a whole and how they are likely to react – will they be embarrassed and disown the interrupter, or take this as the signal for a free-for-all? It should also depend on my knowledge of the particular child, his probable motivation and reaction to different levels of admonition. Is he a constant seeker of attention? Is he deliberately annoying me in order to increase his prestige among his peers? Could it even be that he has a quite justifiable grievance over the inordinate length of time I've taken marking the books?

This is the sort of way that I can give reasons for how I handle the incident: I use my knowledge of the pupils to inform my perception of the meaning of their behaviour. Do my reasons *determine* how I act? The answer is that they do, but not in any way that supports the determinist's position. A person who can give me convincing reasons for following a certain course of action will exert a powerful and probably decisive influence on me, but he does so by requiring me to attend to the facts of the situation and what is known or believed about such facts. He refers me to a dimension where alternative descriptions and reasoned disagreement are always possible, and it is this possibility which affords a kind of freedom that could not exist if we were always at the mercy of environment or heredity.

I have been concerned to emphasize that failure to take seriously the whole business of giving reasons is tantamount to neglecting or at least radically undervaluing the process of reasoning, of thinking carefully about our actions. Taking reasons seriously is intimately linked with trying to perceive the world more justly and so to acting in ways that are more appropriate. People who think we can replace all discussion of our reasons for our behaviour with accounts of its alleged causes are making a crude and dangerous mistake. The particular danger as far as this book is concerned is that they would deny us one of the most powerful ways we have of making ourselves better teachers and perhaps, even, better persons.

2

Classroom Skills and Management

I argued in the previous chapter that we become more effective as agents in any part of our lives when we are prepared to think about our actions, to consider what they count as, amount to or mean. One way of putting this was to say that we need to be clear about the reasons for what we do. The purpose of this chapter is to consider what counts as becoming a more effective teacher and to evaluate the reasons for equating an effective or good teacher with one who, in the fashionable terminology, possesses the classroom skills to manage his pupils successfully.

Now reasons are not abstract or anonymous things: they are reasons for people. When we weigh up what is offered to us as a reason why we should act in a particular way we do not scrutinize its intrinsic quality as a reason in isolation from everything else. We consider how it fits in or fails to with the rest of our commitments and attitudes. What may count as a reason for you, with your set of beliefs and attitudes, the way you feel about the world, may not count as a reason for someone with a very different set. The fact that Peter has shouted a rude word at Alan in the playground in the heat of the moment may strike your colleague as a reason for punishing Peter while it may not seem to you a reason for taking any action at all. You, it may be, are inclined to worry more about physical abuse than the verbal kind, or you think sexual epithets are harmless in comparison with racial ones. If your colleague is to persuade you that Peter ought to be punished he will have to address himself to beliefs such as these, while if you are going to persuade him you may have to confront his tendency to find obscenities disturbing or shocking.

When we give people reasons, then, for following a different course of action or for pursuing their existing goals in a different way, or when we think of reasons for ourselves why we should do

14

this or that, those reasons have to be reasons for persons with certain feelings, beliefs, attitudes and values. Those beliefs and values are likely to be deep and to be related to each other in complicated ways. To fix and make more memorable this rather abstruse point, to which I shall return in Chapter 10, we can summarize it thus: people have depth.

The importance of 'depth' will become clearer as we examine the school of thought that sees the activity of teaching as greatly facilitated by, or perhaps consisting wholly in, the exercise of 'skills'. At the present time there is a heavy emphasis on the skills approach to teaching, matched by a tendency in other areas of education, notably further and vocational education and courses under the auspices of the Manpower Services Commission (MSC), to talk in terms of the teaching and learning of 'basic skills' or 'social and life skills'. It is interesting to consider briefly the reasons for this. In the case of MSC initiatives it is tempting to see the shift to 'skills' as part of the attempt to remove a large portion of the teaching and training of young people, especially those above the compulsory school-leaving age, from traditional educational institutions and put it into the hands of other agencies, which happen to come under a greater degree of control from central government. Or, to put it less cynically, talk of 'skills' recognizes the greater relevance to many young people of 'curricula whose objectives have been primarily derived from a real or imagined analysis of the social demands made on people at work and in the everyday requirements of life in the community rather than curricula whose objectives have been primarily derived from the basic tenets of . . . academic subjects' (*Developing Social and Life Skills*, FECRDU, 1980, p. 6). I shall return to discussion of these sorts of skills later.

In the context of teaching similarly the notion of a skill has a reassuring air of practicality about it. It suggests there are down-to-earth things for good teachers to be getting on with in much the same way as there are for plumbers or dentists. On the other hand a 'skill' does not sound so severely practical as to be mindless: we admire the skill of a surgeon, for example, which comprises knowledge and understanding of an intellectual sort as well as manual dexterity (cf. Wragg, 1984, pp. 6–7). Thus 'skills' have the great merit, from a propaganda point of view, of sounding like a golden mean between extremes: between the purely cognitive or academic and the mechanical, between mere theory and 'tips and wrinkles'.

But although the terms 'skill', 'skilful', and so on are attractive ones at first glance they need to be approached with care. There is a danger of sliding between two senses of them. First there is the sense in which teaching can be said to be a skilled activity, or the country can be said to need skilful teachers, where this means simply that teaching is difficult and has to be learned and that we need teachers who have learned how to teach rather than ones who have not. Claims made in this sense, in which to do something skilfully means little more than to do it well, are, I think, uncontroversial. The second sense, however, is one in which to say that a teacher is skilled is to mean that he has acquired a number of distinct, separately identifiable skills: to say that teaching is a skilled activity is to mean that it can be broken down into these individual skills, with the implication that the best way to learn to teach is to acquire as many of the skills as possible. It is clear that to agree that teaching is a skilled activity in the first sense does not commit one to the thesis that good teaching is most sensibly regarded as some kind of collection or combination of separate and distinct routines.

It is this second interpretation of what it is for teaching to be skilled that has been gaining ground recently. It is prominent in a number of official and semi-official publications, notably the DES Teacher Education Project Focus Books. *Class Management and Control* (Wragg, 1981), for example, lists among other skills those of getting lessons off to a good start, changing smoothly from one activity to the next (called 'transitions') and using praise, criticism or reprimand appropriately ('response'). *Effective Questioning* (Kerry, 1982) includes among questioning skills 'timing' (waiting long enough for answers) and 'reinforcement' (praising good answers). In his summary of the findings of the Teacher Education Project, Wragg (1984, p. 8) characterizes these sorts of skills as 'not so vague as to defy analysis, nor so minute and piddling as to be silly'.

An important question is begged here. Is the best way of understanding complex activities, in this case teaching, always to analyse or break them down into components? This is a relatively modern assumption, and not necessarily a correct one. It owes much to the growth of the physical sciences and their tendency to describe the nature of things in terms of their chemical or molecular structure. But there are other models of understanding than the analytic one. If I show you some unfamiliar object (an old-fashioned gentleman's smoking-cabinet, for example) it is not enough that you can correctly describe its size and shape and tell me what it is made of. To understand what it is you have to grasp what it is *for*, how it is used and how it fits into its context: how, in this case, it implies leisure and perhaps surplus money on the part of a privileged class. To borrow Mary Midgley's terms (1980), understanding, especially the understanding of human behaviour, is often profitably conceived as a matter of understanding what company that behaviour keeps, how it is related to other aspects of the behaviour of the creature concerned.

16

Part of the trouble with the skills approach is precisely that it ignores so much of the context in which teaching takes place. For example, acquiring many of the skills described entails having one's lessons observed by others, such as practising teachers or college tutors. The difficulty here of course is the anxiety such an exercise generates. How many trainee teachers could confidently invite an outsider to observe and comment on their early mistakes, especially when in many cases these will be the same people who will assess the trainee's suitability to qualify for the profession? The skills approach however treats the context as unproblematic: the Teacher Education Project Focus Books blandly instruct their readers: 'Do not feel threatened when these observers offer you advice'. It is not simply that this is to ignore the shortage of confidence which some individuals may be unfortunate enough to suffer from. It ignores the larger fact that teaching is a job usually pursued in isolation and that the development of greater mutual co-operation, supportiveness and trust is a problem for the profession as a whole.

Our feelings, attitudes and so on, then – our qualities as a person in depth – are part of the context in which we teach and cannot be regarded as an irrelevance. Many teaching 'skills' just cannot be separated from the context of wider attitudes and values. I have already mentioned the skill of 'response', which is described as that of using praise, criticism and reprimand appropriately. This clearly goes to the heart of a person's values and beliefs. Do you consider it appropriate to praise for his helpfulness a child who tells you who it was that broke the window, or are you inclined to reprimand him for being a tell-tale? Do you criticize the marks that are still below the rest of the form's, or commend them for being at least higher than last time? Do you reprimand the child who whispers the right answer to his distraught neighbour during a test, or make it clear he deserves some credit for not turning a deaf ear to a classmate's distress? I suggest that developing the 'skill' of praising and reprimanding appropriately must necessarily involve consideration of one's fundamental aims and values as a teacher and a person. Ashton (1982) reaches a similar conclusion, writing that

> skills developed, and the ways in which they are used, directly reflect the kind of person one is . . . For a student to understand his skills development properly, he must be enabled to relate them to his predispositions, his personal constructs, his frames of reference, for skills are not separate and uninfluenced by these, they are determined by them.

The tendency of the skills approach is to proceed as if the teacher in his classroom could exercise a set of techniques susceptible to being 'sharpened' or 'honed' to result in better teaching, without thought of whether these techniques really are educationally desirable or can be separated from matters outside the classroom. For example, Kerry (1982, pp. 35 ff.) thinks that higher-order questions should be designed to provoke increasingly abstract thinking, on the grounds that abstract thinking is the mark of 'high-level understanding'. This is questionable. Is abstract thinking necessarily 'high-level' and therefore, presumably, most desirable from an educational point of view? This would mean that a philosophical treatment of power and corruption, say, was inevitably on a higher intellectual plane than the less abstract handling of the same topic in Orwell's *Animal Farm*. It is not obvious that this is so. Kerry adopts as the underpinning for his analysis of questioning skills a pyramidal picture of knowledge, with information or data as the base, concepts as the second layer and 'principles or abstract entities' as the highest. Why should he do this? There are obvious shortcomings in such a model: for example, information or data will not be understood at all unless they are simultaneously conceptualized. Perhaps the answer can be found in Kerry's *Teaching Bright Pupils* (1981) where he adopts the same model and comments (p. 18): '[This] system is a useful one because it can be applied to a transcript or tape of a lesson to examine the thinking skills demanded by the teacher's talk, the thinking skills evident in pupils' responses to questions, or the demands on thinking skill made by a task.' It is hard not to conclude that the writer's first priority has been to find a model of knowledge that will fit his need to construct a hierarchy of 'thinking skills': the requirements of *analysis* have become paramount and the aims of education are being chosen to suit the skills approach rather than the other way round.

Our classroom practice is quite properly coloured by our views of what is educationally worthwhile – what sort of knowledge is most desirable, for example, or what is the right balance between co-operation and competition. Where we do not attend consciously to the question of the ends or purposes of education our practice in any case reflects conceptions that we have picked up without realizing it. We cannot shuffle off responsibility for thinking about these issues. It is no escape to say 'but I just get on and teach the syllabus': it is the way in which the syllabus is taught that reflects the teacher's wider assumptions about education and teaches his pupils broader lessons about the world. Even a syllabus of sufficient tightness to constrain me to give a vocabulary test on Monday mornings does not tell me whether to trust children to mark their own answers, their neighbours', or neither, nor does it tell me what to do about those who score low marks. From my decisions on these matters children learn about trust, about competition, about what *kind* of failing (laziness? lack of intelligence?) is worthy of punishment. We cannot make any easy distinction, as teachers, between those narrower matters of syllabus and overt curriculum which we will attend to and the wider issues which we will not. We cannot limit the notion of education so as to exclude considerations of, say, justice and fairness: children will learn that we believe certain arrangements are just and others unjust whatever we do. So it is absurd to regret that the issue of whether to segregate 'bright' pupils 'is rarely debated on educational grounds alone' (Kerry, 1981) or to denigrate your opponents as 'those who hold socio-political rather than educational ideals to be paramount in the classroom' (Kerry, 1982). Children learn social and political lessons all the time in schools. For a teacher or educator to pretend they do not is to evade his responsibility for deciding just what he does want them to learn in this area.

Similar criticisms can be made of many of the attempts to promote training in 'basic skills' or 'social and life skills' for young people. Bernard Davies (1979) quotes some striking examples from literature produced by the MSC and related bodies of how the relation between skills and personal qualities such as feelings and attitudes is taken as unproblematic or reduced to the banal. Like trainee teachers, young workers are supposed to be able to pull out of a hat the confidence to report a problem to their supervisor, as if this would automatically lead towards a solution. The business of reflection, which we might imagine to be one of the principal ways in which people come to fit skills into the context of their lives as a whole, is reduced to a matter of realizing 'that if you get your left hand lower down the shovel (if you're right-handed), you'll be able to get a better lift' (quoted by Davies, p. 6). As far as the question of what ultimate ends these skills serve is concerned, recent literature tends to contain soothing statements such as 'the emphasis throughout is what it ought to be, upon personal development of the student' (*Basic Skills*, FECRDU, 1982, p. x) but to give the game away with remarks like 'employers require from young people certain attitudes as well as conventional skills . . . thus . . . attitudes as well as conventional skills should comprise the basic skills we seek to inculcate in young people' (p. iii). Lastly, it is a commonplace in recent criticism of the MSC that it avoids basic social, political and economic questions by treating unemployment as though it is a problem which the individual suffers from because of his personal inadequacy and thus is to be remedied by teaching him the skills of being punctual and coping with interviews.

An adequate critique of the issues involved here would have to address the whole technocratic, utilitarian bias of much recent writing about education in general: in particular the tendency to see education as the acquisition of generic learning skills, transferable from one context to another in the service of the current needs of society, instead of as some kind of good in itself. To do justice to these issues would require another book. For an interesting recent discussion, see Ruth Jonathan (1982).

Because the skills approach neglects the question of the ends of education or treats it as uncontroversial its proponents are apt to make analogies where ends, and means too, are more straightforward. Most of the Teacher Education Project Focus Books tell the reader to work at his skills 'like a craftsman'; Docking (1980) dismisses criticism of the skills approach by comparing the skills of teaching to those of football. I hope there is no need to labour the point that what constitutes a well-made pupil is less clear than what constitutes a well-made bookcase, and that while to be a successful footballer just *is* to have most of the skills of trapping, passing and heading the ball the same is not true of being a good classroom teacher. A person who had mastered all the teaching skills the manuals describe but who had no warmth at all towards children and no real love of his subject or of learning might be a rather dangerous person to let loose in the classroom.

Analogies are slippery things: there follows one of my own. When children learn to read they can be described as acquiring a number of skills. To take just two examples, they learn phonic skills – the relating of sounds to symbols and combinations of symbols – and they learn the skill of recognizing individual words as wholes. As a result methods of teaching reading have been developed which lay heavy emphasis on one or another of these skills ('Phonics' and 'Look and Say'). But we have to ask whether the behaviour of a successful reader is helpfully regarded as a collection of such skills, and whether with reading, as with any other complex activity, the most sensible way to teach it is to break it down into constituent skills and then teach them separately. It can plausibly be argued that when we read we grasp the meaning of a passage of writing more as a whole, and then go back to particular words we have not understood, thus all the time relating words to the wider context in which they occur. Frank Smith (1971, p. 166) writes:

> Meaning identification does not require the identification of individual words, just as word identification does not require the identification of letters. Indeed, any effort on the part of a reader to identify words one at a time, without taking advantage

20

of the sense of the whole, indicates a failure of comprehension and is unlikely to succeed. In the same way any endeavour to identify and perhaps 'sound out' individual letters is unlikely to lead to efficient word identification.

If this is so a child who is more or less instinctively reading for meaning in this way may be badly confused if he is required to switch his attention to individual words and their phonic elements.

The point of the analogy, of course, is to suggest that it may be similarly misleading to direct the teacher's attention too narrowly to individual skills. In particular it may make it harder for him rather than easier to develop a coherent idea of what ends he is working towards, of what the enterprise as a whole amounts to. It is interesting to find that ends are prone to be redefined by those over-impressed by reading 'skills', just as we saw earlier with Kerry's 'thinking skills' and the nature of knowledge. I have heard teachers defend 'Look and Say' methods, with a heavy emphasis on flash-cards, on the grounds that to read a familiar story, for example a version of 'Jack and the Beanstalk', where recollection, pictures and context supply rich clues to individual words, is cheating: *real* reading is being able to recognize 'am', 'here', 'the', and so on in isolation without any context. It is arguable that, on the contrary, literacy even of an elementary level (or perhaps especially at such a level) involves all sorts of things other than merely being able to decode written symbols: it involves understanding a wide range of empirical, social, moral and subjective matters, so that a child learns to read best where his learning draws on the context of this existing understanding.

One way of not losing sight of the complexity of the processes of reading and teaching is to maintain a lively sense of what are the *ends* of these activities, of what they aim towards. I put it like this because there is a tendency to suppose that consideration of ends is some sort of optional extra in teaching and education: that it can be pursued, if it is pursued at all, separately from the important practical business of acquiring skills. Thus the Teacher Education Project Focus Books consign questions of ends or principles to a section entitled 'Reflections', so separate from the rest of the book that, they suggest, such questions might in concurrent courses be studied a year after the 'skills workbook'. By contrast I have argued that we need to devote *continual* attention to what a complex activity amounts to, to what are the ends or principles implicit in the most highly developed or fully realized forms of the activity. It is only this which can guarantee that we are still engaged in the activity itself rather than some simplified substitute which not only misses the point but also may actually prevent us ever seeing the point: identifying words out of context rather than understanding them as *part* of contexts, making smooth transitions from one classroom activity to another with no thought of whether these routines are educationally worthwhile at all.

Further encouragement to leave aside thoughts of ends arises when the teacher regards himself as essentially 'managing' his pupils. For a manager is one who 'treats ends as given, as outside his scope'. His concern is with techniques, with means and their relative effectiveness for achieving predetermined ends (MacIntyre, 1981, p. 29). The frequent conjunction of 'management' with 'skills' is thus the strongest inducement to lay aside the question of what ends the skills serve, what exactly they are skills in *doing*. It is interesting to consider further why talk of management and its skills should have become so fashionable. MacIntyre (ibid.) thinks there is a connection with emotivist theories of ethics. To hold as an emotivist does that people engaged in moral argument are really doing no more than registering their personal approval or disapproval of various courses of action is to leave no room for rational discussion of ends. I may, for example, support a woman's right to abortion under certain circumstances while you believe the foetus has rights which cannot be overridden: on the emotivist theory all we are saying is something like 'this position appeals to me – let it appeal to you!' There are powerful reasons for rejecting emotivism, not least that as a matter of fact we do seem to be able to find a lot of reasons for our views on issues like abortion. Otherwise it is hard to see how numerous books and articles could be written on the subject. At any rate, where it is more or less assumed that no sensible discussion can take place about ends, that we simply have to work towards the given ends of the various systems and institutions in which we find ourselves, we are left with only one criterion for our actions, and that is whether they are suitable means for those predetermined ends. This, of course, is precisely the realm of management and its skills: the economical devising of means for established ends, a business commonly regarded as immune from criticism other than on the grounds of 'effectiveness' if, as emotivism would have it, the choice of those ends themselves is just a matter of individual taste or preference. The question of ends apart, however, 'effectiveness' just is not, as MacIntyre (ibid., p. 71) points out, a morally neutral term in the way that management enthusiasts require it to be. It is bound up with a way of regarding human relations in which manipulating people into compliant ways of behaving is thought acceptable. I return to the topic of manipulation in the next chapter.

One reason why the notion of 'management' and its skills is an attractive one to some people is no doubt that management has a cool, unemotional ring to it, deeply reassuring to those disturbed by the strong currents of feeling in the average classroom, by the aggressiveness or overt sexuality of some adolescents, by the endless haranguing, reprimanding and punishing that fill many teachers' days. Management seems to promise a calmer atmosphere in which pupils could be organized with the same clinical rationality as the items in the store cupboard. It is dangerous, however, to do this in a way that excludes consideration of feelings from education and schooling altogether (cf. Hannam *et al.*, 1977, p. 83: 'The suppression of feeling sometimes seems almost one of the undeclared aims of the secondary school'). For as I argued at the beginning of this chapter, feelings are an important part of the wider context in which teaching takes place. Education is a transaction between persons who have depth, and we ignore at our peril the role of feelings, the affective dimension to that depth. We have already seen how the same attitude to feelings has proved damaging to reflection about ends, for such reflection is held by emotivists to be *merely* the expressing of feeling. The word 'merely' is richly suggestive of the low status feelings have come to occupy.

Probably one reason why feelings are often regarded as having no place in education is that we tend to think of them as blind, uncontrollable surges that just wash over us as they will, rather discreditable and certainly ineducable elements in the lives of creatures who are supposed to be rational. But this is a false picture. Our feelings may be based on a rational understanding of the world: I feel less hurt when I realize you did not mean to speak unkindly to me. And feelings, as I have already pointed out, enter into reasons: your saying that a nasty accident has happened round the corner is only a reason to take a different way home for a person inclined to feel upset by such scenes. It is not a similarly good reason for someone of a morbid disposition.

Perhaps the affective dimension of being a teacher will become more widely acknowledged if we come to accept its importance in learning, and particularly children's learning: the greater readiness with which children tackle intellectual tasks when they arise in a context of human purposes, intentions and feelings with which they are familiar, and the difficulty they experience when required to cope with problems which are not embedded in such contexts. Margaret Donaldson, who has recently drawn our attention forcefully to these factors (Donaldson, 1978), makes the point that teachers and researchers need to be sensitive to the fact that it is precisely the quality of being 'disembedded', not rooted in familiar, affectively coloured patterns of thinking, that makes the development of abstract intellectual powers a matter of such difficulty for many children. This sensitivity is unlikely, I would say, to be found in those who have been positively encouraged to undervalue the subjective, the emotional and the reflective in their acquisition of 'teaching skills', who in their eagerness to learn how to manage others have never seen it as a part of their task to learn to manage themselves.

The discussion in this chapter and the previous one points to the following conclusion. A free person needs to step back from his actions and reflect on what they amount to, what ends they propose. He needs to scrutinize the reasons why he does what he does. Such scrutiny involves asking himself why certain reasons strike him as good reasons, which in turn leads him to consideration of his feelings, attitudes and so on. For reasons are reasons for him as a person in depth with particular beliefs and ways of feeling about the world. (This does not mean that reasons are wholly subjective things: it can be argued that creatures like ourselves, committed to communication and to co-operation in a world of scarce resources, ought to have certain feelings and attitudes and that there are others, such as belief in the law of non-contradiction perhaps, that they cannot avoid having.) This 'stepping back' and reflecting on ends, reasons and feelings is depreciated in much of what has been written lately about the work of the teacher and in emphasis on skills in education in general.

As far as learning to teach is concerned, when proper weight is given again to questions of what our aims are (and what it is possible and appropriate for *us*, being in depth the persons that we are, to aim to do) then I think there will be everything to be gained from closer attention than in the past to questions of *how* to do it. But to concern ourselves with questions of the second sort alone is to devalue the dignity and freedom of persons, as I shall try to show, and pervert the whole enterprise of education.

3

The Teacher–Pupil Relationship

In the previous two chapters I discussed the activity of teaching very much from the teacher's own perspective. The point of view now shifts more to the teacher–pupil relationship and what pupils learn from experiencing different versions of that relationship. Underlying the chapter is the following consideration: if it is so important for teachers, and people in general, to be able to step back and reflect on what they are doing, with all I have suggested that that involves, ought we as teachers not treat our pupils so as to help them to do the same? What sorts of teaching styles does this imply, and which does it forbid?

My discussion of management invites the obvious rejoinder that it is only when the classroom is properly managed, when the teacher is master of the appropriate skills and techniques, that proper teaching and learning, or any worthwhile relationship between teacher and pupils, can take place. Michael Marland (1980) puts this strongly:

> The paradox is that good classroom management makes *personal* teaching possible, for it frees the individual from constant conflict, and only then can the teacher be truly personal. Good organisation in the classroom avoids confrontation, and allows the teacher to establish the warm relationships with most of his pupils that he wants.

This is hard to disagree with, and I am not suggesting that what Marland says is any the less true or important for containing the word 'management'. We can take his point that a disorganized teacher is unlikely ever to arrive at the position where he or she can put any higher-sounding conceptions of teaching into practice at all. But there is still something dangerous in the idea that managing or organizing can actually be separated from teaching and learning: that we can *first* manage the class and *then* get on and teach it what we want. It is dangerous because of the constant tendency for the managing to determine the style and even the content of the teaching. For example, many teachers over the years have (perhaps quite unconsciously) found that a class taking dictated notes is necessarily quiet and passive, and so come to incorporate this procedure more and more into their lessons. Similarly, beginning a lesson with a test is a well-established way of making it clear at the start who is in charge, who asks the questions and takes the initiative: who 'defines the situation', as it is now often expressed. In these examples the teacher may come to teach in a particular manner as a way of managing the class. The trouble is of course that the technique which is effective in managing the class – in keeping them quiet and amenable – may be a poor one as far as actually learning anything is concerned. Few would claim that much real learning takes place through or as a result of the dictating of notes.

Managing simply cannot be separated off neatly from teaching and learning, for the reason that I touched on in the previous chapter: children learn all the time from the different ways in which we manage, organize and control them. If teachers manage their classes by imposing rigid routines children are likely to learn slavish dependence and lack of initiative. Anyone who has found a new class more concerned with the question of where precisely to put the date, and whether to underline it, than with the content of their work, will know what I mean. If we keep our classes under the most constant surveillance throughout their lessons they may well learn to regard themselves as people who cannot be trusted to work in a more relaxed atmosphere, with the result that they never will. If we persistently reward good work with gold stars there is sound evidence (recently from Margaret Donaldson, 1978, p. 115) that children will quickly learn to work for the sake of the stars and not for the intrinsic interest they might have found in the work itself. It might just be, of course, that we had such important academic lessons to teach pupils that we were willing to accept the sort of learning in the three examples above as its price. I shall have more to say later on this point. Here I want to insist only that the way we treat children is itself something that they learn from, and therefore cannot be regarded as distinct from or a mere preliminary to teaching and learning proper.

'Management', like 'skills', is an ambiguous term. There are senses of it which are hardly sinister: if I ask a colleague how he is managing with his third-year class I am not implying he is a proponent of the management techniques which I wrote of in

Chapter 2. Similarly it is possible to observe that good classroom management improves teaching, where this means that forgetting to bring chalk and issuing impenetrably obscure instructions is likely to turn the lesson into a shambles. Perhaps this is the sense in which Marland intends his talk of 'management' (above) to be taken. However at one extreme 'management' shades easily and inconspicuously into something more like 'manipulation'. Children stand to learn all sorts of different things from the various ways we manage our teaching: management of the manipulative sort, I shall argue, is incompatible with educative learning.

Manipulation, as Glover (1970, pp. 155 ff.) observes, is a term with a wide application, used to describe things as diverse as bribery, blackmail, advertising, propaganda and behaviour therapy. As I understand it, to manipulate someone is to bring non-rational, usually covert, influences to bear on them, rather than to show them good reasons for a course of action. Advertising, for example, often works by association of ideas, linking a particular model of car with images of success and sophistication, rather than by making specific claims whose soundness can be tested. A manipulator also works to give his victims new aims or wants in order to further his own ends, as when an unscrupulous politician works voters up to fear some enemy or threat in order to get himself elected through being regarded as the person best able to deal with the problem. Usually a manipulated person has no way of knowing what is causing him to act in the way he does, though it is possible to think of exceptions to this. I might be aware that my boss has made me feel insecure in my job precisely so I will be readier to do what he wants, but still I might find it very hard to resist this sort of pressure.

On this account of manipulation a teacher is manipulating his pupils when, for example, after collecting in equipment at the end of the lesson (perhaps with some difficulty) he announces cheerily, 'Good, now we've got all the magnets back', where his intention is to finish the lesson on a note of satisfaction and send pupils out with the sense that they belong to a well-run class so that they will come in with more positive attitudes next time and be easier to teach. Here the attitudes the teacher is trying to engender are not actually justified by much that took place in the lesson. The means of influence is covert and of course it is the teacher's own ends that are furthered. A second example: it seems to me manipulative to use stimuli which are entirely external to the learning task in hand in order to get the task done: to appeal to the competitive instinct, for example, to hurry pupils through a grammatical exercise in French is not to show them good reasons for learning the grammar in the way the teacher might if he pointed out that by learning the grammar quickly there will be time to read the whole of an interesting passage (that is, one which the class genuinely thinks looks interesting), which requires knowledge of those grammatical features, before the lesson finishes.

In characteristically operating through concealment or sleight-of-hand, manipulation differs from naked authoritarianism. Children who are told to do something and given as a reason the facts that the teacher says so and they will be in trouble if they disobey are at least left in a position to be well aware that their behaviour has been influenced. Successful manipulation, such as the praise given deliberately to promote greater keenness, actually depends on children not realizing that their behaviour is being deliberately moulded. The difficult pupil whom the teacher makes a point of passing a personal word with by the door as he comes in for each lesson must not perceive that this is the reason why it is done; the class which is regularly settled by finding a simple piece of work waiting on its desks is less likely to settle if it realizes that this is the prime or only purpose of the exercise. No doubt it is not possible for teachers to make all of their intentions transparent to all of their pupils all of the time. Sometimes perhaps this is not even desirable: I return to this point at the end of the chapter. But teaching which relies heavily on manipulation will make it impossible for the pupil ever to reflect on the process of his education in any realistic way, for this would expose the subterfuges through which his schooling is run. Such reflection, like the teacher's reflection on his fundamental ends that I wrote of in Chapters 1 and 2, is not a self-indulgent luxury. To devote some thought, such as one's age and capacities permit, to what exactly is happening during the business of being at school and to how one feels about it, to the ways in which one learns best and so on, is to take steps towards becoming a freer and more committed learner. Learning to think about his learning is essential for a person who is ever to be able to take ultimate responsibility for his own education.

In case this reflecting on one's own education and schooling sounds abstruse and philosophical, not a possibility for every child, consider the story of Timothy, a furry animal-infant who sets off eagerly for his first days at school until depressed by Claude, who mocks Timothy's clothes, does not make mistakes in his work and has lots of friends. Eventually Timothy is cheered up by Violet, who is having the same problem with Grace: '"She sings. She dances. She counts up to a thousand and she sits next to me!"' . . . On the way home Timothy and Violet laughed so much about Claude and Grace that they both got the hiccups' (*Timothy Goes to School*, Rosemary Wells, 1983). For a small child, reading the story of Timothy or,

28

more likely, having it read to him, just *is* to be taking one step back from the experience of coping with the pressures of school and to start reflecting on that experience. At a more sophisticated, but hardly unattainable, level Richard Hoggart (1970) describes the following insight into the nature of education:

> I remember once, when I was in the Upper Fifth, for some reason he marked or looked at a set of essays. I had written one on Hardy and had begun it, 'T.H. was a truly cultured man . . .' He stopped me a day or two later, swung against the door of his study, and said, 'What is "a truly cultured man", Hoggart?' I was baffled. I thought he was playing me up, because if our headmaster didn't know what a truly cultured man was, if the phrase wasn't absolutely cast-iron, where were we? And he said, 'Am I one? I don't think so. I don't feel myself "truly cultured".' This was my first sight of a mind speculating, of thought as something disinterested and free-playing, with yourself outside it. I usually thought of a master as somebody who said, 'This is what the such-and-such verb is, or this is what happened in 1762, and you have to learn it'.

The distinction between manipulative and non-manipulative relationships is often expressed, in terminology deriving from Kant, as the distinction between treating people as means, that is as instruments in the working out of some purpose of one's own, and treating them as ends in themselves. To treat a person as an end in himself is to regard him as one who must ultimately take responsibility for his own destiny. It is usual to connect it with treating a person as a rational agent, and here there may seem to lie a difficulty. For children, it might be thought, are not fully developed as rational persons, and this may seem to justify manipulating them, treating them as less than fully rational, on occasion, for their own good. This raises the question of paternalism, to which I return in Chapter 9. At this point I only want to observe that to treat someone as a rational being does not have to be interpreted as a matter of giving him full and adequate reasons, of a necessarily abstract and sophisticated sort. Of course if a five year old asks why he should not run up and down the aisle while his sister is being married it is impossible to give him full reasons in that he cannot be expected to understand what a church is or the nature of a religious ceremony. But this does not mean that no explanation can be given. In such situations we can for example remind children how they feel when something they care deeply about and are concentrating on is interrupted. Analogies, fairy-stories, tales like *Timothy Goes to*

School and parables are just as much part of the flow of ideas between rational beings as the 'scientific' explanation in terms of volts and resistance of why it is inadvisable to push toys into power-sockets. I am not claiming that we owe children explanations on every occasion that life throws up: there are limits to patience as well as to ingenuity and no doubt one of the lessons we have to learn is that other rational beings can often be too tired or in too much of a hurry to give us explanations at the time we want them. But I see no justification for consigning children in general to special, non-rational status of a sort that permits us to manipulate them, to treat them as means and not ends, at will.

It is a little unnerving to think what our pupils will make of our teaching if they are allowed to reflect on it. So it is, perhaps, that we prevent them having time or opportunity for reflection, filling all the available minutes of the school day with what John Holt (1969 and elsewhere) calls 'busywork', the incessant tasks that seem to have no virtue but that of keeping idle hands from mischief. Where children are given work to do supposedly on the grounds that it is necessary for their education but really simply as a means of controlling their behaviour and making life easier for the teacher such 'busywork' must be counted as a species of manipulation. This kind of manipulation is not always wholly deliberate: we tell children, quite correctly, that the work is necessary if they are to pass the test or examination, contriving by a process of double-think or self-deception to forget that often it is we the teachers who set up the hurdles they have to jump. 'Busywork' is prevalent throughout the formal education system. Trainee teachers, who are often obliged to man a production-line turning out files, workcards, visual aids, portfolios and lesson plans, are especially liable to suffer from it, as if to ensure that they will pass it on in turn to those they will themselves teach. The words of a late Victorian public school master are still pertinent to the modern teacher:

> The great lack in a schoolmaster's life is time for recollection and repose. He spins along like a busy top from morning to night, and it is easy to think that if you have spun and buzzed through the hours you have done your duty in a weary way; but there is very little of the feeding in green pastures and leading forth beside the waters of comfort, and the result is that we consider our problems hastily and scantily; we consider prompt action invariably better than quiet reflection. And indeed we have most of us time to do the one and no time at all to do the other. (A. C. Benson, 1902)

30

It is curious that we are inclined to value being busy almost for its own sake and to depreciate 'passivity'. For many people whom we tend to respect as 'active' are, when we think about it, just responding frenetically to external pressures: ridden by anxiety, perhaps, driven by ambition or envy of others. In such cases 'the person is the slave of a passion, and his activity is in reality a "passivity" because he is driven; he is the sufferer, not the "actor"', (Fromm, 1961, p. 21). When these non-rational forces are instilled in us by others for their own ends – when parents or teachers, out of vicarious ambition or to bring credit on themselves and their school, succeed in producing a scholarship-winning child only at the expense of leaving him neurotically compelled to compete against other people for the rest of his life – we are not so much 'active' persons in charge of our own destiny, the 'self-starters' that commerce and industry often advertise for, as the chronic victims of manipulation.

In manipulation the connection between the means by which a person is manoeuvred into doing something and that something itself is purely arbitrary or 'contingent'. If a teacher gets his pupils to learn vocabulary, say, by setting up elaborate competitions and prizes there is no essential or intrinsic connection between the means and the end: threats, punishment or endless drill might have done just as well (or as badly). It is because the means is not linked necessarily to the end that it is liable to break loose completely and become virtually an end in itself, as in the case of 'busywork'. When we give people rational grounds for doing something, by contrast, the means is not logically separable from the end. For example, where the class becomes interested in how French children's lives compare to their own the teacher might ask them to learn some vocabulary so they will be able to understand more of the film French family life they will be watching later. Here the means, pointing out that learning the vocabulary will help them follow the film, and the end, knowing the vocabulary for understanding the film, are not wholly separable, for the means makes reference to the end and vice versa.

There is a constant tendency in formal education for the means–end link to become contingent. This, I suppose, is because we rarely feel able to trust our pupils to want to learn for the right reasons, which must be that what they are studying is interesting in itself, or helps them to a better understanding of the world they live in, or leads to qualifications that employers can be expected to value. And if we do not expect them to be able to see the intrinsic point perhaps this is partly because we the teachers do not always have a clear picture of it ourselves. I find it disturbing, for example, how many graduates training to teach seem to have no grasp of what part their subject can play in drawing a child, or an adult, to a fuller and richer understanding of his world. Thus a graduate in English, asked to describe what he thinks is most *interesting* about Shakespeare's *Julius Caesar*, instead of mentioning that it is about perennially important and absorbing subjects like ambition and power, may immediately talk of the problematic relation between the play and its principal source in North's *Plutarch*. The educational point, to put it briefly, has become lost among the trappings of scholarship, or the imitation of them. To return to the point I made earlier, is there such important *academic* work for pupils to do that we are justified in adopting almost any means, however arbitrary and contingent, for making them do it? Or is it rather the case that the study of literature, history, science and so on is supposed to be *the* way through which an individual comes to understand his culture and society and his place in it? If education is first and foremost coming to understand what is going on in the world around us then it is paradoxical, to put it mildly, to employ devices for getting children to engage in education that operate through concealment and subterfuge: that are designed to *prevent* children understanding exactly what is going on.

Besides 'busywork' and the other kinds of manipulation I have mentioned there are other ways also in which we too readily allow the means–end link in teaching to become a 'contingent' one. There is a constant temptation for the teacher to turn into a showman or performer, relying on unexplained or dazzling effects to maintain order or to capture and hold the attention. I recall a chemistry teacher who inspired awe by writing on the blackboard with one hand, conducting the experiment with the other and simultaneously questioning the class on a different topic. Sometimes teachers become masters of educational hardware, the stars of entertainments featuring the slick use of overhead projectors, tape–slide sequences and computer graphics. These remarks may seem to fly in the faces both of received wisdom and common sense. Children admire a skilful teacher, it is said, and there is nothing like the chaos that descends when the teacher's despairing twiddlings reveal he does not know how to operate the video recorder. The importance of being able to handle the equipment or carry out the routines you choose to use is obvious enough, though the reason perhaps is less that such skilfulness is admirable in itself than that incompetence conveys to pupils the impression that you could not really be bothered about them. Being competent however in employing genuinely suitable means for bringing about worthwhile learning is quite a different matter from elevating the use of means, whether of mechanical

32

equipment, or gesture, or voice, or visual aids, into an act of its own, governed by the criteria of an entertaining performance instead of the criteria of educative learning. (I suspect a good deal of the responsiblity for popularizing the model of the teacher as performer may lie with those educationists, such as lecturers in colleges and university departments of education, who return to the classroom for only half a day or so per week. Partly because of the pressure, in view of their status, to be obviously impressive, and partly because of the impossibility with such artificial and infrequent contact of basing teaching on proper relationships with pupils, such educationists often develop an excessive regard for the showier aspects of classroom teaching, and become fond of describing 'twenty devastating ways to begin a lesson' and similar techniques.)

As teachers we are too inclined to see our work as what Holland (1980, p. 17) calls 'a species of causality – a device for doing something to someone': as a matter of *doing* things to pupils, subjecting them to various processes the result of which is to *make* them compliant and ready to absorb knowledge. It is so natural to us to think of the teacher as somebody who knows more and is therefore a proper person to be moulding or influencing his pupils. That is why it is important not to lose our grip on the idea of education as a rational process and not a causal one, a process that transforms the sense people consciously make of things by offering reasons rather than one which simply implants wants, aims and beliefs by any means that happen to lie at hand. I say more in Chapter 5 about the need for *reciprocity* in the teacher–pupil relationship and for the receptivity on the part of the teacher that this implies. It is worth pointing out here that if we take seriously the idea that pupils are learning all the time about matters like justice and fairness from the ways we treat them our concern that they should be learning aright requires us to be highly attentive to how their views on justice and so on are being modified by their contact with us. Needless to say (I hope), we cannot expect to discover what they are learning on this level by setting them tests, essays and examinations. Under those conditions pupils and students tend only to produce what they believe are the 'right' answers. Because they are so wary of anything that looks remotely like assessment it is very difficult to discover what pupils are learning in any but the most trivial sense. It requires trust and confidence on the part of a child before he can communicate with a teacher about the things which really concern him; it requires the teacher to listen, to attend and to accept, without an eye on how the child's deeper concerns can be harnessed in order to motivate him the better.

A receptive teacher is not 'busy'. (How badly we are teaching children who eventually have to say, 'I didn't like to ask/to come and tell you, I know you're busy.') In fact he or she is 'patient' in the sense of that word in which its etymological connection with 'passive' is prominent: ready to receive experience, to listen and attend. The difficulty of holding on to the idea of receptivity in a world which values the showier forms of activity, of busily doing things to people and managing them, is illustrated by the fortunes of the word 'patient' itself. For to say a teacher needs to be patient would today be widely taken as meaning he must be prepared to keep on trying if he does not at first succeed in getting his pupils to do what he wants them to do.

My discussion of manipulation and what I have written about the value to a pupil of reflection on his own schooling and education suggest that there is another virtue besides receptivity that should be at the centre of the pupil–teacher relationship: that is 'openness'. Someone who teaches in an 'open' way obviously does not use the subterfuges of manipulation but attempts to offer children honest reasons for undertaking study. 'I know it's not very interesting but it's on the syllabus and I shall be in trouble if we don't cover it' is, it should be noted, an honest reason if not a very inspiring one. I am well aware that it is often quite hard to explain what can be interesting or rewarding in the work proposed, but it is usually possible to explain how interesting and rewarding work later depends on foundations being laid. But this had better be both true and to the point. It was really no use generations of Latin teachers explaining that five years' trudge through the grammar would bring its reward in the joys of reading Virgil when most of their pupils knew they would be giving the subject up long before that moment came. Perhaps if we were more accustomed to trying to bring out what is of interest and benefit in what we are teaching we might be readier to abandon those areas of subjects or of the curriculum which children *never* seem able to find in any way rewarding but which hang on through inertia.

There is a political dimension to 'openness'. Ought not open relationships between pupils and individual teachers be matched by similar openness in the way the school as an institution relates to its pupils and, indeed, to its teachers? I mean that there is a case for admitting pupils and teachers on to the school's decision-making bodies and giving them a say in how the school is run, instead of decisions on everything from policy on streaming to details of school uniform being handed down to them from some unchallengeable (and scarcely imaginable) source on high. Pat White (1983) makes the point, which I have touched on myself, that

34

as well as learning their French, maths, environmental studies and so on pupils are also learning how their particular school is run. They are developing conceptions of authority, power, what it is to be responsible for something, what are considered appropriate decision-making procedures and so on. (pp. 92–3)

If children are always necessarily learning some political lesson or other we would do best to bring the whole question out into the open and ensure that 'we can defend our decision-making procedures and the roles and statuses we assign to different members of the institution as the ones most suitable for a school in a democratic society' (ibid., p. 93). Since this issue is treated much more thoroughly by Pat White than I could possibly attempt here I am happy to refer the reader to her interesting book for further discussion.

There are a number of possible objections to what I have written about openness and receptivity, of which I shall briefly consider two. First, concerning openness: education, it may be said, should not aim to make everything explicit. Education is in part a *concealing* process, like art, leaving unsaid and unrevealed gaps into which a person can expand. The deeper satisfactions of education come unbidden to the individual who is obliviously absorbed in his work rather than restlessly searching for its point: 'If joy is to come, it comes as ideas do: by stealing up on us, the entire mind prepared by understandings concealed from mind itself' (Rieff, 1973, p. 190). So it is that since the time of Socrates some teachers have used devices such as obliqueness and irony which have the effect of holding different possibilities open, rather than always 'giving a straight answer' (cf. Thrasymachus' accusation of Socrates, Plato, *Republic*, 337A).

I think there is much truth in this. Not all justifications can without loss be couched in terms of spelled-out reasons. I return to this point in Chapter 5. But the demand for openness in teaching is not a demand that everything should be explicit, only that teachers should neither deliberately use concealment and subterfuge to impose their will on pupils nor be unable to give any kind of truthful answer to the question, 'Why are we doing this?' A truthful answer here is not always a straight answer: it may be indirect and roundabout in its attempts to draw lines of connection between what the children are studying and their deeper interests as people struggling to make sense of their world. In giving such an answer the teacher may try to lead them to the point where they make the ultimate connections themselves; perhaps he *must* do this. Irony and obliqueness are not manipulation. When Socrates said he did not know what justice is and could not produce the 'right' answer his listeners were puzzled and sometimes angry, since he was clearly much more knowledgeable about justice than they. But his irony consisted, not in shamming ignorance when he knew perfectly well (*pace* Lee's translation of *Republic*, 337A, 1968, though perhaps Lee is trying to bring out Thrasymachus' failure to understand Socrates' 'irony'), but in refusing to do violence either to the complexity of the subject or to the need for educative teaching to be *dialectical*, a true and open interchange involving the 'teacher' responding to his 'pupils' rather than just 'telling them many things'.

Secondly, it is by no means the case that receptivity is to be the teacher's first consideration at all times. In particular there are occasions, such as when meeting a new class, when a certain measure of briskness and forcefulness is in order, or the situation in which patience and receptivity can be employed will never be reached. In the short term we often have to adopt strategies that are unattractive in themselves if we are ever to realize our long-term goals, in teaching as in everything else. But that is simply a further reason for not losing sight of what those ultimate goals or ends are. Each individual teacher has to exercise his practical judgment, in the particular circumstances he finds himself in, on the question of what compromises, what means, are acceptable: but he can do this only in the light of an adequate conception both of what end he is trying to reach and of what the compromises cost. It is the nature of the ends and the cost of the compromises that I am trying to show.

4

Authority

One reason for the popularity of the managerial, manipulative philosophy, I suggest, is the ambivalence commonly entertained towards the idea of authority. On the one hand there is, as is often observed, widespread rejection of more traditional attitudes of deference: that a person in authority should automatically be respected, that authority should command ready obedience and have appropriate sanctions at its disposal to deploy against the recalcitrant. We dislike what we think of as authoritarianism, with its implications of overbearingness, browbeating and bullying. Yet on the other hand we cannot deny the need to prevent chaos, in the classroom as elsewhere. We tend to think that this is the teacher's function and that he or she is justified in creating conditions in which their voice can be heard. And so we welcome the techniques of the managerial repertoire which seem to promise order without, so to speak, orders.

This is why it is so important to maintain a grasp of what is the proper work of the teacher. We have already seen some of the limitations of the manipulative style of teaching and the solution to the problem of authority which that represents. I shall argue in this chapter and the next that the nature of the teacher's work also precludes certain kinds of authoritarianism yet at the same time shows that we cannot eliminate the notion of authority or something like it from teaching altogether. Thus the purpose of this chapter and the next is to explore further the nature of the teacher's proper work, just as the last one held implications for the nature of authority. There is no tidy division of the subject-matter between the chapters.

I make this point because some readers may expect to find an 'analysis of the concept' of authority, or even an 'investigation of ordinary usage'. I must say, without digressing into the complex question of the nature of philosophical method, that I consider the view of philosophy encapsulated in those phrases to be inadequate. Of course it is necessary to distinguish importantly different kinds of authority and to expose any confusing ambiguities in the use of the word. But I doubt if we can sensibly talk of *the* concept in cases like those of authority, freedom or discipline, where the words themselves have propaganda value and constantly find themselves borrowed to lend respectability to widely different, and even opposed, moral and political programmes. As it is sometimes put, these are 'essentially contested' concepts, ones which are the battleground over which philosophical and ideological dispute takes place. We should not expect to find such a thing as the uninfected usage of ordinary, disinterested speech which can be neutrally analysed. Our understanding of the nature of authority is not advanced only through philosophy of the linguistic analysis school. Far from it: Shakespeare is writing about authority in *Measure for Measure* and so is Virgil in the *Aeneid*. Such writers, like some philosophers, deepen our understanding of authority by showing in detail the interconnections between its different forms and other aspects of our lives: our feelings, our personal relations and our public institutions. Here it is the links between the business of teaching and authority in its various guises that I shall try to explore.

It is probably as well to recognize at the start that there is no shortage of people who would regard the very enterprise of questioning the notion of authority and bringing it into philosophical discussion as more or less subversive, a symptom in itself of all that is wrong with education (and perhaps the world) today. Such people often maintain that authority, by which they usually seem to mean persons invested with formal powers, such as headmasters and policemen, ought automatically to command respect and obedience. They speak with horror of 'abdication of authority' where a teacher, say, suggests that the answer to certain sorts of questions is less straightforward than other people think, that the quality of children's work cannot always be assessed in quantifiable terms, or that some transgressions against school rules are better overlooked than punished to the letter. Carroll (1979) expresses something like this viewpoint: 'That we can doubt that education must by its nature be based on authority, the authority of the teacher and of the tradition he passes on, is indicative of the demoralisation of our culture.' Such a viewpoint may be more sophisticated than the simple conviction that people just ought to do as they are told. Three reasons in particular are often advanced in support of the claim that schoolchildren especially ought to respect authority.

38

First, 'Authority is necessary in education because students crave it . . . All men to a greater or lesser degree long for authority' (ibid.). This invites several rejoinders. The fact that people crave something is not in itself a reason why they should have it. It might, obviously, be bad for them, or they might be mistaken in their identification of what they want. Then too there seems no reason why Carroll's claim should be confined to pupils: teachers must be given the security of being told what to do by headteachers, headteachers by advisers and the Inspectorate, and so on. I hope the absurdity of this is obvious enough. Furthermore we can ask what distinguishes the beneficial security which authority allegedly confers from the lifeless rigidity of a classroom where children feel secure simply because the only demands made on them are entirely predictable and they are permitted to run no risks.

Secondly, it is sometimes said that the requirement for children to respect and obey authority in school is justified by the existence of the same requirement in the world beyond, for which it is the function of the school to prepare its pupils. Bantock (1952) writes that 'the school necessarily involves an authoritative set-up'. Amongst other justifications of this he offers the following: 'Power is an inescapable element in adult life, to which we all at some time or other have to come to terms'. This raises the important question, to which I shall return, of whether authority and power are quite the same thing, as Bantock here implies. It also raises the question whether schools are to be seen essentially as places where children are prepared to fit in with the demands of the outside world. Might we not also want them to an extent to be places from which children go out to make the world *different*, juster or more free or more compassionate? The future is not wholly predetermined. Today's children will shape it into whatever it will be. This is a logical point, not merely an idealistic one. If schools are to train children to defer to authority such deference has to be justified on better grounds than that we find a lot of deference in our contemporary culture. We find crime and vandalism in the world outside the school too, but this does not justify us in preparing children to be criminals and vandals.

Thirdly, emphasis is sometimes placed on the notion of obeying authority, or following rules, *as such*, where the point of adding 'as such' is to exclude obedience due either to the influence of the particular person issuing the order or rule, or to perceiving the point of the rule, the good reason why it has been established. John Wilson (1977) believes that without the notion of 'established and legitimate authorities as such' no institution or society could rely upon anything but *ad hoc* bribes or threats to get things done. It is easier to see what (I think) Wilson has in mind here by looking at a rather different sort of case, that of moral duty. For me to experience the urge to, say, visit a sick friend as a genuinely moral duty my motivation must be uncoloured by what philosophers since Kant have tended to call 'heteronomous' considerations, considerations that is such as expectations of some advantage accruing to me from doing what I know I ought. Similarly the specifically moral worth of my doing my duty is lost if I do so because some third party shames me into doing so and I make the visit because of his influence rather than because of the pure claims of duty. I must, that is to say, feel the promptings of duty *as such* if my action is to have *moral* worth. It is not necessary to go into the reservations that can be expressed about this rather austere doctrine to see that it undermines rather than supports Wilson's case. For where I perceive a moral imperative as authoritative or a moral rule as binding I do not perceive it as authoritative or as a rule 'as such', as though there were no more to be said of it than that it was a rule. By identifying it as a *moral* rule or as an imperative speaking with *moral* authority I indicate the area, in this case the moral one, from which the reasons that justify the rule or command are drawn. And though it may be true that we cannot give reasons for moral rules that justify them in terms of their consequences, whether for the agent or anyone else (for on the Kantian account that would detract from the specifically moral worth of compliance), it does not follow that no kind of elucidation at all can be given. It might be possible, for example, to display the nature of virtues like justice or patience in such detail that their moral value was self-evident, as Plato has Socrates attempt with the nature of justice in the *Republic*. We use such devices as examples and parables for the same purpose.

In this way moral rules can be explicated and moral authority can be understood: the specifically moral element in them, which is what gives them their point, can be drawn out and made clearer. If it is moral rules and authority that Wilson has in mind, then, when he writes of the importance of acquiring a notion of authority and rules 'as such', he appears to be wrong. And his claim is even less plausible in the case of other sorts of rule or authority. Where we abide by the school rules or the rules of a game or accept the authority of the traffic-policeman there is simply nothing that can count as doing so out of respect for rules and authority in themselves. What makes a rule a rule rather than the expression of a wish, or an order or a means of coercion pure and simple, is that it is neither particular nor personal in its nature. A rule forbidding running in corridors applies to all relevant persons in all corridors at all times: it neither specifies the particular individuals by name who are to comply, nor does it derive its obligatoriness from being enforced by this person or that. It does not cease to be a rule when the school is empty of the teachers who normally ensure it is obeyed, nor when the headmaster who added it to the school rules retires. It is the non-particular, non-personal nature of the reasons for the rule that we grasp when we are following a rule. To understand that we are confronted with a *rule* is already to understand something about the reasons why we should follow it. A rule is not a kind of direction which we can first recognize and later, perhaps as an optional extra for especially sophisticated persons, consider the justificatory reasons for. Unless we are capable of perceiving that the reasons are of a certain sort we cannot think of it as a rule at all. 'Never go near the fire' is not a *rule* for a child who merely keeps away from the fire because he associates it in a Pavlovian sort of way with a smack from mother. He begins to conceive it as a rule when he grasps that there are reasons for him not to go near the fire and sees that those reasons are not based on a whim of mother's nor apply only to him but to those who are relevantly like him. (He would not articulate his growing understanding in this way, of course.) The same is true of obeying authority. I can be said to accept the authority of the policeman when I understand that he has reasons of a certain sort for telling me not to park here. That is what distinguishes accepting authority from simply obeying out of fear of the consequences of not doing so, whether those consequences are delivered through the accepted legal procedures or not.

To sum up this point, I do not think that any sense can be made of the idea of obeying rules or authorities 'as such', and I agree broadly with Straughan (1982b) who writes:

A child can *either* conform to the edicts of some personal source of power and influence, *or* he can appreciate the reasons which justify an edict and accordingly make it authoritative rather than merely authoritarian. In neither case, however, is he obeying rules or authorities *as such*, for in the former he is simply doing as he is told, perhaps with no idea of what constitutes a rule or a legitimate authority, while in the latter he is doing what he sees there to be good and sensible reasons for doing.

Authority has *grounds*, some sort of rational justifying basis which can be indicated. This, broadly, is how exercising authority is different from wielding power.

At this point it may occur to some readers, if it has not done so before, to wonder whether the simple fact of having been formally

41

invested with certain powers itself constitutes an adequate basis for authority. Does not the fact that a teacher, properly qualified in the eyes of the DES, has been appointed to his or her post by a board of governors (or whatever the correct procedure is), mean that they have sufficient grounds for their authority? There is a connection here with the idea that authority must have a rational basis, for the teacher is appointed, ideally at least, because his own educational attainments, his references and the qualities he displays at interview reveal that he has the appropriate qualifications to exercise authority: intellectually and morally he is the sort of person to have good reasons for what he says and does. In practice of course it is not as straightforward as that. That a person occupies a particular office may perhaps create a strong expectation that he will act with good reason, but it is clear that the reasonableness of his behaviour is logically separate from the formal position that he holds, and it is with reference to the former, to whether his pronouncements, decisions and actions really are based on adequate grounds and reasons, that his authority is justified or not. If this were not so it is hard to see how we could ever be justified in questioning, let alone opposing, the decisions taken by someone who is properly authorized, in legal terms or the terms of the constitution of a school, university or any other institution, to make decisions or give orders.

That we must reserve the right to examine critically decisions made by those in positions of authority is made clear by an argument which Plato has Socrates use in the first book of the *Republic*. Socrates' opponent, Thrasymachus, had asserted that justice, or, roughly, what is right, is simply whatever the powerful decide is right. No other meaning can be attached to the notion of just or right action, he thinks, than whatever accords with the will of those individuals who are in a position to impose their will on others. As far as authority is concerned this would amount to saying that what is ordained by those in formal positions of power is simply to be identified with what is right, so that there are no independent grounds or standards to appeal to, except of course the pronouncements of those in even higher positions of authority. It is worth noticing that on this view we can speak of power and authority interchangeably: there is no basis for distinguishing them. Indeed, this is one way of expressing Thrasymachus' claim. However the claim cannot possibly be true. As Socrates points out, the powerful can be mistaken, about what is in their own best interests as about anything else, so that if what is right is what the powerful ordain it will sometimes be right to do what turns out to damage their interests, even when this was not their intention. This shows that we cannot eliminate the distinction between what is really in someone's interests and what he merely thinks is and so authorizes to be put into effect. In other words, we find that we are forced to accept the idea of a set of standards of what is right independent of what any particular person or group of people declare is right. We can see the same point if we consider our reaction to receiving, from a properly constituted authority, an instruction that makes no sense or contradicts itself. That we can recognize it is meaningless or self-contradictory shows that we cannot do without some conception of standards which transcend the will of particular individuals, some notion of the impersonal authority of certain rules of correctness over and above the authority a person has in virtue of his position or formal status. This is not to suppose that there exists some *particular* set of immutable, eternal standards or laws, writ in the heavens or elsewhere. It is only to insist that the notion of rightness goes beyond and cannot be reduced to what any person says is right.

Philosophical argument demonstrates that there can be rational grounds for dissenting from the word of those invested with formal authority: history shows the importance of never forgetting the argument. There have been, and still are, many regimes where the legitimate authorities command actions that (whatever our political persuasions) we tend to feel their subordinates would have done better not to carry out. We are not very impressed by the defence offered by those who deported Jews and others and destroyed them in concentration camps, or those American soldiers who murdered innocent civilians in Vietnam, that they were only doing what they were told. We admire those who, despite the cost, disobeyed because they owed allegiance to the authority of higher principles, whether moral, religious or humanitarian. As we might expect, there is evidence that even those with good reason to object to the orders of those in positions of power find it difficult to make a stand if they have a history of ready deference to formal authority and its trappings. John Benson (1983) cites Bruno Bettelheim's study of the way prisoners in the concentration camps of the Third Reich responded to their conditions:

> People from a social class in which external badges of status were important, who depended on the respect and approval of their fellows, were quick to succumb when deprived of these props, 'which had served them in place of self-respect and inner strength' . . . some adopted the outlook of the SS and tried to get accepted as their loyal subordinates.

This suggests that even in cases where we personally find the commands of formal authority congenial it is important to keep a grasp of the good reasons that make those commands rationally defensible. For what people who believe their power is the only measure of justice sometimes come to require of those subject to them is, not to comply through seeing the sense and the point of their commands, but simply to obey, without thinking, so far as possible, at all. George Orwell makes this explicit in *Nineteen Eighty-Four*, his satire on authority that takes this shape. Syme, a colleague of the hero, Winston Smith, perceives that the Party, the rulers of the state of Oceania where the novel is set, have one purpose in their systematic reduction of the English language: to narrow the range of thought that is possible. Obedience involves, not thinking that the Party is right (for that, as we have seen, would be subtly to introduce a criterion of justice other than the will of the Party), but not thinking at all. '"Orthodoxy means not thinking"', Syme explains. '"Orthodoxy is unconsciousness".'

Where the State sets itself up as the arbiter of all forms of truth – as in *Nineteen Eighty-Four* the Party even claims the right to say what happened in history and whether two and two make four or five, and in the Soviet Union insanity appears often to be established less by purely medical evidence than by what we would call political considerations – we call the result 'totalitarianism'. That is an extreme, political version of *authoritarianism*, which I take to be the view that a person should be obeyed simply because he is in a position of authority, whether this is a legal or semi-legal position like that of a teacher, army officer or chairman of a committee, or one based on traditional status, such as a father or parish priest. (The distinction is not a clear-cut one: teachers' authority, for example, may be thought to derive as much from their traditional standing in the community as from any powers formally delegated to them.) An authoritarian is not someone who occasionally fails to give reasons (perhaps through impatience or lack of imagination) for his decisions and actions: he is rather one who holds that those in formal positions of authority are to be obeyed purely in virtue of that and not because of the reasons that underpin their decisions and actions. When an authoritarian reaches a position of authority he will characteristic-ally not feel obliged to justify his actions with reasons and may be outraged if asked to do so. The second kind of teacher that I described in Chapter 1 is a good example of such a person.

The term 'authoritarian' is usually used pejoratively. Are there any situations in which authoritarianism might be justified? One range of situations of this sort might be those where it is perhaps more important that there should be obedience and discipline in general than that any particular order can be shown to be the best that could have been issued in those circumstances: where the nature of the situation is such that it would be unrealistic and unreasonable to demand reasons before complying. Examples might be a military operation, members of the public following the instructions of the police at the scene of a motorway pile-up, and perhaps footballers following their captain's tactical directions during a game. It may be more important for all the players to follow the same tactics, even if they are not very good ones, than for each to go his own way, and the same applies to the military operation, where it is particularly vital for each soldier to follow his part of the plan and be able to rely on his comrades following theirs. Obeying the police readily at the scene of a motorway accident prevents the chaos and further accidents that would probably ensue if we waited for them to justify their instructions to us. It rightly prevents us from undertaking those calculations of personal advantage which might prove disastrous to others, as when I might think I could find a cheaper breakdown firm than the one called by the police and resent being held over a barrel, but all the while my wrecked car is a potentially lethal obstruction to others. Unsurprisingly, writers who are impressed by the need for authority and rules 'as such' like to compare a school to these 'tightly-structured, quasi-military situations', as John Wilson (1977, p. 44) calls them. Thus he talks of an army, an operating theatre, a classroom and a ship as making the same sorts of demands on people. But it is clear that some of these situations involve urgent life-and-death considerations which on the whole are rare in the classroom. The consequences of a child asking me why I have told him to move to another desk are not to be compared to those of a nurse being disinclined to pass the surgeon the forceps until she has been told precisely what he wants them for. In any case we tend to assume that the surgeon, the policeman and the football captain do actually have good reasons which they could explain and would probably be willing to explain at a better time. These are not true cases of authoritarianism. Military situations are complicated by the almost pathological tradition of taking pride in obeying even (or perhaps especially) when there *are* no good reasons, even when it is known that 'someone had blundered', but still I think that for the most part an officer carries most authority with his men when they know he usually has good reasons for the orders he gives them.

The distinctive feature of 'quasi-military' situations, then, even if they are not always truly examples of authoritarianism, is the presence of some danger or other contingency so pressing that it warrants postponing consideration of reasons and justifications for commands: we do better to do as the relevant authority says before the time has passed by when any useful decision could be made. John Wilson (ibid.) does not explain why a class of schoolchildren and (Heaven help us) a family must be thought of as such tightly-structured, quasi-military groups, and I can see no reason why they have to be so. Of course, we can *make* them thus if we want. We can for example engineer the continual crises that then permit us to point to the necessity for the formal authorities to make *ad hoc* decisions without consultation. For this purpose it is a great advantage for the totalitarian state to be at war, either against another state (as Oceania, in *Nineteen Eighty-Four*, was always at war with Eastasia or Eurasia, and it did not matter which), or against internal elements (Communists, 'enemies of the revolution', and so on). In the classroom the teacher similarly might try to claim that the syllabus has to be covered before the examination, leaving simply no time for his procedures to be questioned and justified. We can sympathize with the hard-pressed teacher here while bearing in mind how easily this can turn into a routine where there is always 'too much to get through', where pressure is more or less unconsciously generated in order to justify avoiding discussion and explanation: not just the 'busywork' I alluded to in the previous chapter but busywork to a deadline. In the same kind of way headmasters may be too inundated with communications from the LEA concerning falling rolls, closures, mergers and cuts to have time to consult with their staff or even let them know what is going on. Much the same is true throughout the education system, where particularly in times of retrenchment it appears that too much has to be decided too quickly for opinions always to be asked and possible courses of action justified or even discussed. So those in positions of power can invoke the existence of crisis to justify requiring compliance without consultation, and if this mode of management is to their taste (for people do not always relish the difficult task of giving good reasons) they have a vested interest in ensuring that the atmosphere of crisis is maintained.

One drawback of authoritarianism which must be mentioned in the context of education is its incompatibility with certain kinds of learning. Obviously enough if children are treated in an authoritarian manner they will learn little, for it is the nature of authoritarianism not to base itself on reasons, and children learn from being given reasons. But authoritarians also cut *themselves* off from learning, from the improvement of understanding that can occur when we test our ideas in public. It is largely through subjecting ideas to open criticism that we discover how to make them sounder. A viewpoint that has not been aired in this way is likely to be marked by its author's limited personal vision, his failure perhaps to consider objections that may be obvious enough to others. And of course when we are dimly aware of the difficulty of defending what we want to say there is sometimes a special temptation to avoid challenge and discussion, to assert and rely on our own status or formal position to carry us through. In this respect authoritarians are like self-deceivers, who, being obliged to ignore evidence that would contradict their cherished beliefs, must discount more and more of the facts of the world around them in order to maintain their version of reality.

Some readers will by now probably have come to the conclusion that I am in some general way 'against authority'. It is true that I regard authoritarianism, and the unthinking acceptance of authority, as great evils. I do not see how anyone with the smallest knowledge of history can take any other view. But it does not follow at all that I imagine it would be possible in some sweeping way to abolish the idea of authority altogether, let alone that I think this is desirable. In fact I think it is quite clear that we just could not do without the notion of something like authority in our scheme of things. The reason for this is clearly put by Winch (1967). Where we take part in complex activities of any sort, whether it is teaching, playing the piano, putting up shelves or whatever, our taking part is bound up with our tacitly acknowledging that some things will count as failing in the activity and others as succeeding. It is hard to see what sense could be made of the statement 'Peter is putting up some shelves' if the speaker set no limits at all to what counts as putting up shelves. So 'to participate in such an activity is to accept that there is a right way and a wrong way of doing things' (Winch, 1967, italics removed). It is not so much that there is *a*, one single, way of putting up shelves or teaching that is the right way and all others are wrong, as that we must with such activities be prepared in principle to make the distinction between right and wrong ways, success and failure. Here we admit the notion of something like authority: the authority of the standards that mark the difference between right and wrong ways of doing things. (I say 'something like' because although I think that we cannot do without the *concept* of authority, for the reasons I have given, it is not clear to me that the *word* 'authority' is really appropriate in all cases of this sort.) I fully agree with Winch's way of putting the matter:

> To submit to authority (as opposed to being subjected to power) is not to be subject to an alien will. What one does is directed rather by the idea of the right way of doing things in connection with the activity one is performing; and the authoritative character of an individual's will derives from its connection with that idea of a right way of doing things. (ibid.)

47

This analysis may sound dry but it is good news for people who like to preserve their independence of mind and spirit: for teachers who like to think of themselves as something more than part of a compliant workforce whose job is simply to implement the latest directives from on high and fall in with current fashions. For since it shows that standards, the measures of rightness and wrongness in activities, are logically distinct from the will of persons it opens the possibility for the individual to pursue his activities with some degree of autonomy: not to have to accept uncritically others' version of 'the right way of doing things' but to act according to such standards as he can find good grounds for, can rationally justify and defend.

5

Justifying Authority

What, then, are the standards by which teachers can justify their
professional behaviour? What is it that the teacher understands the
right way of doing, that makes him or her worthy of being seen as in
some sense *authoritative* in the classroom or the school?

One obvious kind of answer amounts to saying that the teacher
justifies being *in* authority by the fact that he is *an* authority – on
history, geography, mathematics or whatever. There are two
principal variations on this answer, which I shall for convenience
label the 'rationalist' and the 'acceptance' versions.

The 'rationalist' model emphasizes that to be authoritative is to be
able to give good *reasons*. To be authoritative on, for example,
mathematics, then, is to be able to justify one's statements by
reference to reasons based in the logic of the subject or its
fundamental procedures, the distinctive ways of operating that make
it this subject and not another. Giving reasons will be a rather
different business in the various subjects, or 'forms of knowledge' or
'areas of experience', that make up the school curriculum. This kind
of account is at the present time very popular. It has in recent times
been propounded in a very influential paper by Hirst, 'Liberal
education and the nature of knowledge' (1965), and taken up in a
number of official publications such as the Inspectorate's booklet
Curriculum 11–16 (HMI, 1977).

There are a number of problems with this model. First, it is
doubtful whether there really are such different, clearly identifiable
fundamental procedures, such distinct structures of reasons to
appeal to. Rather we find that what is the basic nature of scientific
method or of literary criticism, to take just two examples, is itself a
matter of intense current controversy. Moreover close examination
of the claim that there are something like six or seven distinct forms
of knowledge or reason-structures, corresponding (conveniently) to
the basic subjects of the school curriculum, has led some writers to

49

conclude that there are either only two distinct forms or structures or considerably more than half-a-dozen, perhaps a limitless number, depending on the criteria used for making the distinctions. (See, amongst others, Barrow, 1976, Pring, 1976, and Watt, 1974.) Secondly, even if there are such procedures and structures it is implausible to suppose that the average teacher has as philosophical an insight into the nature of his subject as the 'rationalist' model seems to require. Few science teachers, for example, appear able to discuss the methodology of science beyond a very elementary level. It is arguable, of course, that they are none the worse as science teachers for that.

Bantock characterizes the view that the child must be shown the nature of what he is studying and the reasons why he is studying it in similar terms as a 'rationalist assumption' (1952, p. 194). So far from regarding the teacher as being an authority in being able to give reasons of this sort Bantock thinks this view is one of the main forces tending to 'destroy the notion of authority in human affairs' (ibid., p. 187). It is worth noticing that an influential version of the 'rationalist assumption' has recently re-emerged in Bruner's claim that any subject can be taught to any child at any stage of development in an intellectually honest way (Bruner, 1960). But Bantock rejects the 'rationalist' model on quite different grounds from mine. He seems to think that there *are* identifiable 'good reasons' for, say, studying particular subjects or areas, but that children, by virtue of being children, are unable to understand them. This leads him to embrace the 'acceptance' model, echoes of which can be found in many school staffrooms. He holds that schoolchildren are confronted with the unknown of the subject or area of study, which requires them to make a 'leap of faith'. Before any learning can begin they must simply accept the authority of the teacher, who is therefore an authority in the sense that he possesses knowledge beyond the present grasp of his pupils. They are in no position to understand any justifications he might offer for calling it 'knowledge' rather than just something he felt inclined to assert.

If all this is correct then neither the 'rationalist' nor the 'acceptance' models of what it is for a teacher to be an authority in his teaching hold out any hopes that he can justify this *to his pupils* in a way they can comprehend. We seem forced back again to a more authoritarian view of the teacher's work.

However it is interesting to take one of Bantock's examples at this point, the study of Classical Greek. At first sight this, being *par excellence* an esoteric and remote subject, appears to illustrate his claim. 'How is it possible', Bantock asks, 'to *explain* to the normal urban-bred grammar school child, with the culturally impoverished background that so many of them possess, the importance of the study of Greek . . .?' The question-begging word here is 'explain' which, especially in its original italics, seems to suggest the supplying of clear-cut, logically irreproachable reasons of the sort we give when we say 'If you move your knight there then he'll bring forward his bishop and then it's checkmate next move', or 'The coolest part of the house in summer is usually the ground floor, because hot air rises'. Here the reasons do belong to a generally accepted structure of reasons to which appeal can be made in case of doubt or dispute. But not all reasons are of this sort. ('I can't explain. You'd have to know him to see what I mean': cf. Iris Murdoch, 1970, p. 33.) We can justify without giving the kinds of explanations we do in the case of chess, geometry or physics, and it is a mistake to think that these areas supply us with the model to which all explanations and justifications must conform. To return to Bantock's Classical Greek, it is possible to introduce children to the Classical world through its myths, legends, art, history and literature in translation. Through such an introduction they may begin to perceive some of the pleasure and the point (and perhaps the pleasure, or a certain sort of pleasure, *is* part of the point) of studying the culture of ancient Greece and so they may see value in learning the language that would give them more direct access to it.

This shows the possibility of giving explanations and justifications without clear-cut reasons of the sort that are in place in chess or geometry, which I shall henceforth call 'explicit' reasons. The same possibility can be seen in other areas of teaching: in the way, for example, that a teacher is likely to justify his judgement that a piece of writing is 'sentimental'. Of course he is likely to indicate which are the passages or phrases which he would say particularly display this quality, but beyond that there really are no 'explicit' reasons to give. His justification will probably take the form of trying to expand his pupils' conception of sentimentality so that they come to see his judgement as well grounded. To this end he might for example show them other pieces of writing where this quality or its opposite are much more obvious. Nor need we regard a justification which takes this form as necessarily second-best to, or as a replacement for, one couched in terms of 'explicit' reasons. Imagine, for example, trying to help children perceive that war is not all glamour and glory. Reading Wilfred Owen's poetry with them, or Remarque's *All Quiet on the Western Front*, or arranging a showing of Renoir's film *La Grande Illusion*, is not some sort of poor substitute for a series of statements beginning 'because'. Such works – poetry, novels and films – have the status they do because they are the best way that exists of understanding the nature of war. Moreover the sort of explanations or justifications which such works constitute is often prefigured in material appropriate for the very youngest children. In trying to explain to a five year old why his younger brother becomes angry and frustrated at being unable to do all the things he can do it is natural to refer to a favourite story in which the same thing occurs. Although this is not the kind of explanation we find in the textbook of child psychology under 'sibling rivalry', none the less it is an explanation of the younger child's behaviour, or a justification of our saying to the older child 'It's only natural for him to be jealous', which I think we have to say is truthful and can be illuminating.

We tend to assimilate all reason-giving to the giving of what I have called 'explicit' reasons, and so we tend to think of reasons in general as if they had some very remote, impersonal and anonymous status: as if the reasons for studying Greek or for calling a poem 'sentimental' just are what they inflexibly are, and we struggle to understand them as best we can. On this view it is natural to depreciate the extent to which teachers and other adults can give children good reasons: to take Bantock's approach and think of the teacher's being an authority as a matter of his simply being at a stage, whether in respect of sheer knowledge of facts or in respect of deeper intellectual development, that children have not reached. One curiosity of this picture is that the more emphasis is laid on the difference in knowledge between teachers and pupils the harder it is to see what could count as helping pupils towards a deeper understanding of anything. They can certainly be 'told many things' by a teacher who is an authority in Bantock's sense: what is the climate of Peru, how to conduct the chemical experiment, how to conjugate the imperfect tense of the French verb. But it is a characteristic of teaching that improves understanding that it must somehow latch on to what is already known, to the child's existing experience in some broad sense. By that I do not mean that only the literature of working-class life is to be read with working-class children or that the kind of history appropriate in the school is always local history. I mean that, for example, a child will make little sense of a novel like *Lord of the Flies* unless he sees, however dimly, that it is about issues already familiar to him: power, loyalty, betrayal. The good teacher brings these connections out, perhaps by working on such topics with the class for a while before even beginning the book. Now the more we appreciate that in this sense children do, indeed *must*, have some understanding already of what *Lord of the Flies* is all about, the more difficult it becomes to maintain that the teacher is an authority in that he has knowledge and the pupils are in a state of ignorance.

It might perhaps be maintained that this is the case in some areas of the curriculum only and that there are other subjects or disciplines where the much greater relative ignorance of the pupil means he has at least to start by taking what he is told on trust. A distinction might be drawn between the humanities, to which we always bring our common understanding of the world, and the sciences, whose procedures and specialized language seem at first sight not to be prefigured in the same way by everyday ideas and ways of thinking. It is in the sciences, of course, that 'explicit' reasons have one of their natural homes. But still the most elementary concepts in physics and chemistry, such as those of mass, weight, energy and valency, have to be explained to children in such a way that they can make sense of them. They have to be related to, and where necessary distinguished from, their existing concepts. Once we get to the stage in science of talking about what counts as evidence for what it becomes yet more clearly true that evidence has to be related to existing understanding. Strike (1982, p. 46) puts the point thus:

> Propositions that are objective evidence for some claim must be subjectively seen as evidence by the student. This requires the student to integrate reasons given by an instructor into the student's current concepts in such a way that they are structured as evidence within the student's cognitive structure. We must remember that a proposition or a phenomenon is only evidence for a claim in relation to a set of concepts that explain it.

The position I have reached in my argument in this chapter can be put as follows. The way the teacher is an authority is not to be regarded as a matter of his simply knowing more than his pupils. They are not barbarians at the gates of knowledge who must put their trust in the teacher's cognitive authority before they can be admitted to learning. The extent to which children already possess knowledge, concepts and understanding and are capable of receiving explanations and perceiving the point of activities forbids this picture. (See Chapter 9 for further discussion of this issue.) Yet Bantock was correct in rejecting the 'rationalist assumption' in that children may well be unable to grasp 'explicit' reasons and reason-giving sequences that consist of 'because' clauses. We pass between the horns of the dilemma – between the horn of 'acceptance' and that of the 'rationalist' model – by seeing that demonstration of the grounds for a claim and justification of what we say can often take other forms than the giving of 'explicit' reasons. And so it becomes possible to maintain that the teacher's being an authority in his teaching depends on his being able to justify what he says in these other, broader and richer, ways. Explaining now looks more like a matter of being able to help pupils to make appropriate connections, between new and existing items of knowledge. For a teacher to be able to do this successfully he clearly must, as Strike (1982) observes, have a rich grasp of 'what the student's current concepts are': he must understand something of *what they are making of* the experiences into which he as teacher is intervening.

It would be wrong to imagine that it is only older children who have built up such complex interpretations of experience. Consider the following example. Two small children, both under five, have been asked to collect some favourite toys to amuse themselves with on a long journey. Looking at what they decide to take – a jumble of model animals, cars, small bricks and so on – a Helpful Adult substitutes items he judges more suitable in having more variety and interest and being less likely to frustrate the children by getting lost on the floor and between the cushions in the back of the car. On the journey the children show little interest in the Helpful Adult's collection. Their mother produces the original selection the children made themselves and they play perfectly happily with them for hours. The point of this story is not just that this was what they *wanted*, but that these toys and knick-knacks, so random and unconnected to the casual eye, were part of an elaborate game, incomprehensible to outsiders, that the children had been building up over some time and were currently obsessed with. This their mother, who was a constant observer of their play, had realized. It was what they were *making of* things, what things *meant* to them, that had to be understood.

The picture that begins to emerge of the process of teaching, as we probe this question of the basis of the teacher's authority, is thus a more and more complex one. It is not just a matter of knowing one's own subject, nor even of understanding it deeply enough to be able to produce reasons for what one says based on its distinct logic or fundamental procedures. Teaching seems to involve understanding what pupils are making of their experience, including their schooling. This is the kind of receptivity or patience that I sketched in Chapter 3. It involves helping pupils to make connections between old and new pieces of knowledge so that they can in the fullest way make sense of what they learn. It involves making contact with children's minds, and through that contact encouraging the interplay, the tossing to-and-fro of ideas between teacher and taught such that children perceive that their existence as individuals with particular interests and difficulties modifies the content and manner of the teaching. The basis of the teacher's authority, then, is that he or she is good at teaching in that wider sense, possessing such qualities as patience and receptivity to an unusually high degree. To bring out the paradox, the difference from the traditional picture, we could say that the authoritative teacher turns out to be good, amongst other things, at attending to his pupils, at experiencing them honestly and accurately.

The discussion so far took as its starting-point the basis of the teacher's authority in his understanding of the subject or subjects he teaches. It may be felt that there is another kind of wisdom that gives the teacher a right to be heard, and that is his deeper moral understanding and his surer moral judgement. This is what justifies him in, for example, stopping bullying, rebuking inconsiderateness, praising honesty and courage. Again we need to consider whether this is a kind of authority that can be justified to children, either by the teacher giving good reasons and explanations for his moral teaching, or in other ways. Here particularly it seems that children stand in need of such justifications, for justifications point to what it is in a piece of behaviour that is praiseworthy or the opposite, such as the motive out of which something was done. It is the intention to spoil a classmate's new bag, for example, that makes doing so morally worse than breaking a window by accident, though the latter may be more noticeable, more inconvenient and, the world being what it is, more angrily received.

Phrases like 'moral authority' and 'moral judgment' ring unpleasantly to some people, to whom they have overtones of repression, of being made to feel guilty or ashamed without good cause. This is not the place to trace the process by which 'moral' has become almost a dirty word (cf. Mary Midgley, 1972). Perhaps those who find it so have come across too many authoritarians of the sort whose fondness for calling behaviour 'immoral' appears to increase in proportion to their inability to produce any good arguments against it. It is important to notice that if moral authority can be shown to have some basis, if moral judgments *can* be justified, then moral understanding is one more defence against authoritarianism: the moral life is an area in which we may be able to come up with better justifications for our actions than simply that we are told to do them by our superiors in some hierarchy.

We justify our moral injunctions in a wide variety of ways. Sometimes we try to show that behaviour, such as cheating, works against the agent's best interests in the long run. Sometimes we appeal to the notion of duty, as when someone who has accepted some kind of formal responsibility fails to discharge it. We may base justification on a wide variety of virtues: those such as fairness, which are concerned with relations between people, those such as proper pride or generosity which are connected with the kind of person we like to see ourselves as, and those such as carefulness which are concerned with the manner in which we do things. This is of course not an exhaustive list of possible moral justifications, nor is it uncontroversial. In particular the distinction between the last two kinds of virtue is far from clear. It is also a vexed question what relative weighting we should give to these different elements in the moral life. Still, it is when we have some understanding of these various elements and can communicate our understanding to others that we can claim our moral authority rests on adequate grounds and show that our judgements and decisions are based on something more than mere personal whims and preferences.

With morality even more than with other areas of understanding we cannot think of children as in a state of plain ignorance and the authority of the teacher or adult as constituted by his simply knowing what the child does not know. Nor can we make the 'rationalist assumption' and think of the justification of morality as a matter of giving straightforward 'explicit' reasons. To take the last point first, our ordinary ways of extending children's moral awareness do not invariably consist of moral judgements followed, separately and distinctly, by reasons. We make statements of the form 'That's wrong because . . .' much less often than we attempt to describe behaviour in such a way that its moral quality is obvious: 'That's bullying', 'I call that cheating, not sharing ideas'. It is not so much that we do not justify our judgements as that we justify them, and the repugnance, approval or admiration that may be part of them, by a description of the relevant action under which we intend the child to recognize what he or another has done. Similarly we say such things as 'You should take more pride in your work' or 'That's hardly fair, is it?' where again we seem to assume that the child has already some existing conception of pride or fairness. This shows why the 'acceptance' model will not do here either. Our justifications function more like reminders of what is already known or half-guessed than as suppliers of fresh, compelling information. (Though of course new information may have an enormous bearing on moral discussion: for example we blame the shoplifter less, or perhaps not at all, if we learn he is under treatment for depression which makes him forgetful.) In this respect 'Don't walk on the ice: it's very thin' is rather different logically from 'Stop looking at your neighbour's work: that's cheating'. Of course we can still think of this re-describing and reminding in moral cases as the giving of *reasons* (this may help us to remember it is not merely the reporting of personal preferences), as long as we bear in mind that reasons function in a different way here from the way they do in the non-moral cases represented by the example of the thin ice.

The teacher is an authority in the area of morality, then, not so much when he has knowledge that his pupils lack as when, first, his understanding of the world is wider and richer than theirs and, second, he has the kind of openness and receptivity that I mentioned earlier. From the first quality he derives, not certain knowledge to communicate, but a wealth of intuitions and tentative insights to contribute to the dialogue between himself and his pupils. The second quality amounts to the willingness to try to understand what his pupils are making of their experience, to help them make connections and find sense and coherence. This is to be a teacher in the manner of Socrates in the early dialogues of Plato (the *Euthyphro* is a good, short example), searching for examples that will persuade your pupils to re-examine their principles, providing anecdotes and stories to illustrate your own, being ready to admit your own uncertainty and fallibility.

If these qualities do not seem very common among teachers one reason may be that phrases like 'moral education' and 'moral authority' seem to push us back towards a more didactic picture of the teacher's work. Too much overt concern for morality, as has often been observed, is not always a morally healthy thing. The phrase 'moral authority' is particularly unfortunate, suggesting as it does that there are persons we might go to for authoritative rulings on what is right and wrong in the same way we would go to someone who was an authority on Regency furniture. This is one of those cases I alluded to above (p. 47), where the *concept* is relevant but the *words* are inappropriate. Here we are discussing what it is for the teacher to have moral authority in the sense of possessing a proper understanding of the moral area of human life. If we throw out the concept – the concept of there being ways in which moral judgements can be justified – through disgust with the wording then we are likely to end up with a conception of morality in which moral judgements are merely expressions of personal feeling: an emotivism which, as MacIntyre (1981, p. 22) writes, 'entails the obliteration of any genuine distinction between manipulative and non-manipulative social relations'. We must hold on to the idea that there are ways of justifying what we do and say morally, even if we do not want to say that someone who is good at supplying such justifications has 'moral authority'.

It is obviously important in the moral area that teachers should be examples or models to their pupils. By this I do not mean that teachers are to be prigs or paragons of virtue, though clearly their authority will suffer if their professed moral views and their own conduct are at variance, nor do I mean that they should tend to draw attention to their own qualities, however genuine and worthy they are. Any self-conscious display of or deliberate search for opportunities to parade moral views and qualities is likely (like separate lessons in Moral Education) to persuade pupils that morality, along with algebra and French irregular verbs, is only to be found in schools. I mean rather that children need to see that morality *matters*, that moral issues are often ones that people care about deeply. It seems to me quite proper that teachers should occasionally be seen to get angry or upset or indignant over a question of moral concern, providing the question really does warrant such feelings. Children would be getting a misleading picture of morality if moral issues were always dissected for them in a cold and analytical way. I remember a class coming into my lesson one day in an unusually serious and thoughtful mood. It emerged that the teacher of the previous lesson, a man seldom known to raise his voice or show irritation – not even at mislaid exercise books or breaches of school uniform regulations – had reacted angrily to the groans and laughter with which the contributions of one unpopular member of the class were often greeted. That this had provoked the rare anger of a person they respected had clearly impressed the children more than any amount of discussion of tolerance would have done.

Of course there are dangers here. Growing tired and impatient we are prone to becoming angry not with the one offence that in our more sensible moods we consider important but with the hundredth trivial irritation whose ninety-nine predecessors we ignored or forgave. That is just confusing for children. We also risk bewildering them if our feelings are such as they cannot comprehend. For example, the intense revulsion that many adults feel towards cases of sexual abuse of children is not something any child, especially before adolescence, can really be expected to understand. No doubt we do best to play down our feelings in matters of this sort. But the general point seems a sound one: feelings enter morality, and a child has learned too little about the moral life if he does not begin to see what feelings are appropriate in various moral situations. This lesson can hardly be learned any other way than by moving among adults who show what it is to experience moral questions as a matter of live concern. Thus 'we learn through suffering': morally we learn in part by truly experiencing our feelings, by attending to them and reflecting on them, on their conflicts and ambivalences, and by living among others who do the same. This marks one limit to the desirability of the teacher taking a neutral stance on controversial issues like abortion or disarmament. Better, perhaps, impassioned one-sidedness that does not pretend to be anything else than a disinterested impartiality which obscures the fact that moral questions matter.

There is at least one other important respect in which teachers need to be a model or example in order to justify their position. It is a fine thing if pupils perceive the possibility of loving what they learn for its own sake, of finding history or mathematics or whatever absorbing to the extent that a person might actually want to go on studying beyond the hours he is compelled to. Here there is no substitute for the teacher as example, as one who loves the subject himself. Certainly any kind of verbal assurance that a subject is enjoyable is likely to be regarded by children as cant, particularly where the pleasure is always located in the future and appears in the light of one more inducement to persist in the drudgery of the present. Of course the point of learning sometimes does lie in the future: pupils often and quite properly study with the aim only of gaining a qualification and where this is so it is no doubt advisable to be grateful they have found something to motivate them. But just as they miss the point of morality if they do not grasp the way feeling enters into it so they miss part of the point of education if they do not perceive the possibility of its being a source of deep and lasting satisfaction. It is worth noting, to balance what I have several times said about the importance of the teacher bearing in mind what children make of their experience, what things mean to them, that a teacher who loves literature or physics or painting shows that his vision extends *beyond* the world of children to something which is what it is whatever they may or may not make of it. The range of this teacher's interests is not limited by the classroom and we might expect his pupils to respect him as a person all the more for that.

Throughout this chapter I have been attempting to relate the notion of authority to those of justification and reasons. To be authoritative is to be able to indicate *grounds* for your actions, decisions and assertions. It is to give reasons, though not all reasons by any means are of the kind I have labelled 'explicit': giving reasons and justifying are more complex and diverse activities than this. I return to discussion of reason and reasons in Chapter 10. Reasons are also important when we come to consider the kind of exercise of authority we call punishment, as we shall do next.

6

Punishment and Discipline

Among those who work in difficult or dangerous jobs, for example in coal-mines, there is often a discipline that comes not from being subject to the will of any person, however rational and well-intentioned, but from the work itself. If it is to be done successfully and with the minimum danger and discomfort to all those engaged in it certain procedures must be followed and safeguards observed. Because the workers can see that the nature of the work demands this there is correspondingly less need for discipline to be imposed on them by some other agency. This is an ideal situation, as far as discipline is concerned: where the discipline is inherent in the work or activity, and where rules or procedures are followed because they are perceived as appropriate if the work is to be done. In the same kind of way it does happen, and fortunately not all that rarely, that a class of pupils appears collectively to accept the idea that learning some arithmetic, say, is a good thing and that if they are to learn then various routines, such as doing the homework set out and not interrupting the teacher when he is explaining a difficult point, have to be kept to.

I am not concerned to argue about the definition of 'discipline'. Some writers would reserve the word for the following of rules because they are seen appropriate to the task in hand (thus P. S. Wilson, 1971) and would reserve the adjective 'disciplined' for the class like the one above but not apply it to a group of pupils which has been brought to order by some external factor such as the teacher's threats of punishment. Other writers take a wider view of discipline in which it is perfectly proper to speak of one person or group of persons being 'disciplined', that is brought to order, by another's imposing of his authority. I think there is nothing to be gained by attempting to stipulate that the word should be used in

60

one way or another. I only want to insist that whatever words we use there is clearly a difference between three sorts of cases: one, where we follow rules willingly because we perceive them as right or appropriate; two, where we follow them under manipulative coercion, such as when we are persuaded that there is no alternative to the rules; and three, where we follow them under what may be called punitive coercion, being threatened with punishment or in general some unpleasant consequences if we do not.

It seems clear enough that the first sort of case, whether or not we call it 'discipline', is what we would prefer to find in our schools. The question of course is what we are to do when this ideal breaks down or has no chance to develop. What kind of action can we take to bring about the order necessary for teaching and learning, and indeed for civilized relationships in general, to take place? I have already been heavily critical of manipulative modes of treatment, yet as I suggested it is likely that one reason for the growth of manipulative practices, particularly in schools, is the feeling that punishment is somehow a bad thing: that it is repressive or psychologically unhealthy, or that to punish a pupil is in itself tantamount to an admission of failure of some kind. Consequently there is, I think, a reluctance in some quarters of the educational world even to think about punishment. Sometimes this is rationalized by saying that anyone who teaches well should have no need to punish. But there can be few teachers who have *never* found themselves forced to issue a punishment. It therefore seems a good idea to devote some careful thought to what is involved in punishment.

Sometimes punishment has been regarded as a practice in keeping with the values most civilized people would probably support. For a start, it can be said to be respectful of the individuality of persons: it is usually individuals that we punish, whereas manipulation and other methods of control characteristically are designed to influence groups. Then too punishment respects freedom: on at least some views of punishment, as I shall describe later, punishment offers us the choice between on the one hand committing an offence and incurring the punishment and on the other observing the rules and keeping our liberty (or our money or whatever). Manipulation gives us no such freedom of choice: it may not even allow us to realize our behaviour is being influenced. Punishment is also connected to the values of justice and fairness: I shall call punishment *fair* if it falls on offenders (as opposed to the innocent) and *just* if it is a response to the breaking of rules which are good and sensible ones. Manipulation however makes no distinction between those who would and those who would not have behaved in the desired way if left to their own devices.

It cannot therefore be assumed from the beginning that punishment is an unmitigated evil, to be avoided at all costs in a community. This assumption is perhaps easier to make because in a wide sense a lot of 'punishing' goes on all the time in ordinary human relationships. That is, we often feel aggrieved by another person and, particularly when they are close to us, we make them suffer in return. Often we do this only half-consciously, dimly feeling that we have been hard done-by and retaliating without being at all clear about what we are doing. No doubt this sort of behaviour is a great evil and source of unhappiness in people's lives. But this wider kind of 'punishing' is not what I am writing about here. The need to distinguish this from the kind of punishment which is the subject of the rest of this chapter and the next two may make a rough definition helpful at this point.

I follow what has become known as the Hart account (Hart, 1968), with appropriate modifications, which I shall defend presently, for the case of schools rather than courts of law. Punishment consists in the intentional infliction of some sort of unpleasantness, by one somehow entitled or authorized to do so, on an offender for a wrong voluntarily done by him. The point of this definition is simply to make clearer the subject under discussion. It is not meant in itself to pre-empt argument or to solve any problems. However it does help to distinguish the sort of punishment I am concerned with here from the sort mentioned in the previous paragraph, for obviously there can be no question of anyone being entitled or authorized to inflict punishment in ordinary human relationships between, say, husband and wife. Beyond this, however, the definition leaves many questions open.

What, for example, is the purpose of stipulating that punishment should only be for offences committed voluntarily? This is certainly the case with the majority of offences liable to punishment under criminal law. There the advantages of allowing it as an excuse that a person did not know he was committing an offence, or was forced to commit it against his will, are, according to Hart (1968, pp. 45 ff.), those of choice and confidence or security. If I am liable to be punished only when I have acted willingly and wittingly then my own choice is effective in determining my future. I assume a responsibility for my own life, and experience the satisfactions of one who feels in control of his own destiny, that I could not have if from time to time I found the course of my life diverted by the requirement that I pay the penalty for offences I did not know I had committed. In addition to this I am thus better able to predict the future with greater confidence that my plans can be carried through.

In schools, on the other hand, teachers do not always feel similarly obliged to establish that offences are voluntary before they punish them. The child's failure to do his homework may indeed be due to factors at home outside his control, or he may quite genuinely have been trying to be friendly rather than insolent to the teacher, but it is the experience of many pupils that they are punished without account being taken either of intentions or extenuating circumstances. Why should this be any more tolerable in schools than it is in the world outside? Admittedly teachers do not have the resources for making investigations which are available to those who enforce the criminal law, and decisions in the classroom sometimes have to be made quickly. Perhaps, however, this just means that we should not punish unless we are reasonably sure about an offender's motive and the truth of any excuses that are offered. After all, it is possible to require, in the examples above, homework to be produced without fail the following night, when yet another sister's birthday party would be stretching misfortune beyond plausibility; it is possible to have the apparently insolent child stay after the lesson to discuss his behaviour with you. Such measures are often inconvenient for the teacher, but inconvenience has to be weighed against the likelihood of resentment on the part of a pupil who feels his intentions have been misinterpreted.

This is connected with an important way in which punishment in schools differs from judicial punishment in the wider world. Judicial punishment is incurred for an offence against laws or rules, which can be inspected in statute books and elsewhere. The connection of course is that when a person can know in advance, because rules have been published, what he is liable to be punished for it is possible for him to exercise the choice and live in the security that are supposed to be the advantages of order being maintained through punishment rather than through manipulation or sophisticated bullying. In schools, on the other hand, teachers commonly punish pupils for offences that are not expressly forbidden by rules. The danger in this is obvious: pupils may come to feel that punishment is less a result of their own intentions, choices and actions than of the whim of the teacher. Yet it is hardly an attractive solution to increase the number of rules so greatly that punishment can always be shown to be the consequence of breaking an explicit rule. For then children would very likely come to regard the wrongness of wrong conduct as consisting simply in the breaking of rules, rather than in being inconsiderate or endangering the safety of others or whatever it is that the rules are intended to prevent. That is, a heavily rule-bound institution engenders in its members what might be called a kind of moral immaturity in which they cannot see beyond the rules to the reasons for them. Moreover, where there is a proliferation of rules the disregard or even contempt into which some of the petty or trivial ones fall may begin to infect the more important ones. An apparently pointless rule against leaving the school by a certain door is widely ignored, and no one can be bothered to enforce it; then the rule against crossing the main road other than by the footbridge falls into contempt, with perhaps fatal results. It might be some answer to distinguish among the importance of rules by the scale of the punishment. One problem here is that teachers often seem convinced that by mounting a purge against relatively minor misdemeanours they will somehow eradicate the major ones: as if a successful campaign against infractions of school uniform regulations will mysteriously cause general improvements in behaviour. I know of no evidence to support this belief. It seems at least as likely that children will at best resent being harassed over matters they see as of little importance and at worst become seriously confused about whether the length of skirts and width of trousers is more or less central to the proper running of a school than bullying or stealing.

However many rules we have they clearly cannot in any case cover everything for which schoolchildren have customarily been liable to be punished, unless some are catch-alls such as 'Never annoy a teacher'. This of course is precisely the sort of regime which children see themselves as enduring in schools: one where they get punished merely for contravening teachers' wishes, however capricious and unreasonable they may be. Corrigan's study (1979), for example, of adolescent pupils shows the extent to which they saw school punishments as just a matter of their being 'picked on' and 'pushed around', victims of the arbitrary will of the teachers. Here is none of the predictability, the confidence that one's own choice will determine the course of his life, that is supposed to characterize the proper operation of punishment. Catch-all rules therefore seem no answer to the problem of how children are to know what they are liable to be punished for. Might we perhaps simply abandon in schools the connection made in the world outside between punishment and explicit rules? This seems to be the policy of a comprehensive in Essex, which declares in literature sent to prospective parents and staff 'School regulations are kept to a minimum . . . The school demands high standards of work and behaviour . . . any deviation from expected standards comes into the area of punishment'. The wording is unfortunate, suggesting (though no doubt not meaning) that straightforward lack of academic ability may be punished. But an attempt might be made to justify punishing without explicit rules having been infringed in two ways, as far as I can see. First, it might be argued that punishment in the case of children has a rather different function from punishment in the case of adults. Children are less mature and less rational: we cannot assume they know what they are doing in the way we normally can with adults. Children are punished less because they have knowingly broken rules than so that they may know the correct standards in future: punishment thus has a teaching role. I discuss this argument in the next chapter. Secondly, it could be said that in schools established routines can take the place of rules. We are then justified in punishing a pupil who without excuse contravenes a routine we have reason to believe he is familiar with: he enters the classroom when he should have waited in the corridor, for example, or fails to bring the appropriate books to the lesson. Everything depends, of course, on these routines or expectations being made sufficiently clear, as well as the consequences of failing to comply with them. Otherwise there will be nothing to distinguish these routines from others (such as the routine the class has drifted into, unasked, of always sitting in the same desks) where, to borrow the Essex school's wording, deviation does not come into the area of punishment. This is the ordinary practice of many teachers: they establish known routines, rather than publish rules. Punishment of infringements of such routines will certainly meet the criteria of predictability and security that I have mentioned. But these routines are beginning to look very much like rules: the only difference is that they are not written down. Yet clearly it is quite possible for them to be more familiar to children than many articles of criminal or civil law are to the average adult.

It is important to be clear about the direction of the argument so far. I am not claiming that as teachers we are justified in establishing any rules or routines we like and punishing children for breaches of them. Rather my argument is that, when we wish to prevent certain sorts of action (and therefore to promote others), first a case can be made out for preferring punishment over other means, notably manipulation, of achieving our end, and that secondly punishments in school can be relatively like judicial punishments in being incurred only by those who have offended voluntarily against known rules or routines. I have several times stressed that punishments, properly understood, have the advantage of minimizing resentment on the part of the pupil. This is not just liberal or permissive thinking. It is obvious enough that we do not want any devices we adopt for achieving order in schools to end up by increasing disaffection and alienation. Of course even where rules (from now on I shall use this term to include known routines) are well known and offenders against them are punished only where they have done so voluntarily and without excuse it is still possible for pupils to consider the rules themselves trivial, absurd or merely the expression of teachers' idiosyncratic or selfish wishes. The pupils may even be quite right in this. But there is no solution to that problem to be found in the nature of *punishment*, and I think it is a big mistake to put pressure on the notion of punishment in the attempt to make it yield such a solution. For example, P. S. Wilson (1971) tries to ensure that punishment cannot be a means simply of enforcing whatever the teacher likes by tying it logically to specifically *moral* rules, as we shall see in the next chapter. On my account of punishment enforcing a rule through punishment certainly does not guarantee that the rule is sensible or just. Rather, on my view, the merit of punishment lies in the *way* it enforces, in its having, so to speak built-in, the protections such as predictability that I have already mentioned. Arriving at just rules is a different and additional task. A healthy society has procedures for doing so, for challenging unjust rules and laws, and similarly a good teacher explains and discusses rules and routines with his or her pupils, occasionally even changing ones that are objected to with good reasons. Even where rules are unjust the punishment may be fair in being impartial between pupils, in taking account of relevant excuses, and so on.

It is obviously very important that teachers should be clear when they are inflicting, and pupils when they are suffering, a *punishment*, and when something different but confusingly similar is intended. Punishment is deliberately inflicted unpleasantness: it is not punishment if the unpleasantness is incidental. I do not punish a pupil whom I set extra work to improve his chances of passing an examination, however tiresome he finds the work. Nor am I punishing the class if at the end of a lively and enjoyable art lesson I ask them to spend a few minutes making the room usable by the class that comes in there after break. In these cases I must make clear, by the wording of my request, the tone of my voice and so on, that this is not punishment, for the class that made a mess accidentally while working well will very likely resent the implication that they were ill-behaved if they think they are being punished, with consequent damage to our future relationship. There are other occasions which may resemble punishment and must be distinguished from it if punishment is not intended. Reproof may be meant more as a reminder ('You must remember to bring the vocabulary book in future') or in a more elaborate form as an extended telling-off it may be meant rather to cause discomfort and shame, in which case it is surely a kind of punishment. Again a teacher does well here to be clear about his intentions, for the child who experiences as punishment what was intended as no more than a reminder may feel that he has been treated unfairly. Where no distinctions are made it is no wonder that teachers are seen as sources of undifferentiated unpleasantness, fond of 'getting their own back' on pupils or 'throwing their weight around'.

It is particularly confusing, in my view, to attempt to make a distinction between punishments and penalties. Those who do usually claim that a penalty is an appropriate response to a breach of the regulations designed for the smooth running of an institution when no real wrong is done – examples given are often those of fines for overdue library books or for parking on double yellow lines – while a punishment is the reply to significant wrongdoing. Accordingly there are some teachers who like to impose a battery of impositions, unofficial detentions and other minor 'penalties' on pupils who arrive late for lessons, default on homework, forget pens and rulers, and so on. I take it that the point of thinking of these as 'penalties' and the significance of their being imposed often more or less automatically without discussion is to avoid the morally charged atmosphere of guilt and shame that is often felt to surround the notion of punishment. Perhaps that is commendable, but I do not see why we have to think of punishment as inevitably accompanied by a crippling burden of shame and guilt. Nothing in my own account implies this. In any case, the distinction between punishments and penalties seems to me misguided in two ways.

First, where the distinction is made on the basis of the kind of rule breached, as above, it appears incoherent even on its own terms. For why do we 'penalize' the sorts of things we do unless there is something wrong with them? The double yellow lines outside my house are there because the road narrows and bends at this point, and if I leave my car there for the sake of convenience, confident that police or traffic-wardens rarely come past, I am acting selfishly and risking causing an accident. If I keep my one-week loan for longer, deciding it's well worth the fine, I am keeping it from another reader who might well have planned his work on the assumption that the book would be back when it was due. Similarly with offences against the smooth running of the classroom or school: if they really matter, if for example they selfishly cause inconvenience to other people, let us think of the detention or whatever as a *punishment*. Apart from anything else, doing so may help keep before our minds the need to consider motive and intentions. If on the other hand they matter only a little or not at all let us scrap the relevant rule or respond with remonstrance, reminder, reasoning or in some other way. Thus penalties are confusing because they convey the message that the behaviour penalized does not really matter, while the child still finds itself on the receiving end of what looks remarkably like a punishment.

Secondly, recall that punishment is supposed to have the merit of respecting the individual's responsibility, of giving him the choice of whether both to offend and to pay the price or observe the rule and preserve his freedom, so conferring the benefit that he is in charge, in this respect at least, of his own life and destiny. If we make school a place of *penalties*, conceived as being imposed for offences 'which neither you nor your judge necessarily regard as being of any *intrinsic* importance' (P. S. Wilson, 1971, p. 117), we offer children this autonomy while at the same time denying them it. We do not offer children the chance to begin to take responsibility for their own lives if we regard this freedom as extending only over things that do not really matter. This makes school not so much a part of life (and so a place where the world is explored and tested) as an eccentric, self-contained game of its own. For the remainder of this book I shall write of punishments and penalties, punishing and penalizing, interchangeably.

To insist that it is precisely where matters of importance are concerned that people must be given significant responsibility may seem strange in the context of punishment. For it may be thought that what we want to do is to *prevent* crimes and offences, not leave people with the choice of whether to commit them or not. The reader may be inclined to agree with Rawls (1972, pp. 314–15), who declares that punishments are 'not simply a scheme of taxes and burdens designed to put a price on certain forms of conduct . . . it would be far better if the acts proscribed by penal statutes were never done'. Certainly laws and rules are intended to prevent offences taking place: to quote Hart, it is not 'a matter of indifference whether we obey the law or break it and pay the penalty. Punishment *is* different from a mere "tax on conduct"' (1968, p. 44). The point of punishment, however, is that while it aims to prevent offences it does this in a way that leaves room for other principles and goods that we value, which a more single-minded, draconian system of preventing offences would not. To quote Hart again, 'More is at stake than the single principle of maintaining the laws at their most efficacious level' (ibid.). If that was *all* we wanted, we would behave very differently. We might for example take measures to isolate or even exterminate those sections or age-groups of the population statistically most likely to commit crimes; we would no doubt institute curfews and compel people to carry identity cards. If we have reservations about measures such as these it is because as well as freedom from crime we value other things, like freedom of speech, of movement and association. All this applies with equal force to schools, where we value not only obedience to rules but also the individuality, initiative and readiness to experiment that often characterize the process of learning but may conflict with rules being maintained 'at their most efficacious level'.

I have so far been concerned to justify punishment by pointing to the benefits and safeguards that it incorporates. That is one way of justifying punishment: there are other, separate and distinct, questions about the justification of punishment still to answer. In particular there is the question of the purpose or general justifying aim, as it is sometimes put, of punishment. That is, punishment may be a way of achieving a particular end that incorporates various safeguards, but what exactly is the end that it is meant to achieve?

As may already be clear, I accept that the general justifying aim of punishment is to secure greater obedience to laws and rules by deterring offenders, both those who have already offended from doing so again and those who so far have not but might if not deterred. If this seems too obvious an answer to be worth making, I do so at this point because different answers have been offered, such as that the general purpose of punishment is to reform offenders, or to visit retribution on them, or to reveal the moral order. I discuss some of these in the next chapter. Although it might seem that the question of the general justifying aim ought logically to have come first I have left it until now both in order to sharpen the contrast with manipulative means of securing order by indicating the procedural advantages of punishment, and in the hope of minimizing confusion among the various different justifications of punishment. Where an account begins by stating that deterrence is the purpose of punishment it is all too easy to get the impression that this answers all questions of justification. That is why those who regard deterrence as the general justifying aim are often taken to have committed themselves to savage exemplary punishments or to the punishment of the innocent, for the former might deter very effectively and the latter might be necessary to maintain deterrence where for some time no offences had actually taken place (see below, p. 86f).

Deterrent punishments in schools raise a number of further problems, discussion of which I shall also postpone (see Chapter 8). I want to end this chapter by identifying one particular reason why, I believe, many writers are reluctant to conclude that deterrence is the general justifying aim of punishment. This looks like justifying punishment by reference to its beneficial consequences for a society or community, as, in a sense, it is. However to justify a practice solely by pointing to its consequences is regarded by many philosophers as tantamount to removing that practice from the moral dimension of human life altogether. To take an over-simplified example, if I consider myself obliged to keep a promise to you, not simply because I *promised*, but only to the extent that the consequences appear, when I weigh them up, more beneficial to all involved than those of breaking it, then I have failed to understand the specifically moral nature of promising. The obligation to keep a promise does not derive only from the consequences of doing so. To deny this is to be a consequentialist, or perhaps the particular kind of consequentialist called a utilitarian, who holds (again I simplify) that actions are only good or right to the extent that they promote the greatest good of the greatest number of people. Now even where philosophers have been prepared to concede that consequentialism is a moral outlook at all, rather than one actually antithetical to morality, many of them have wanted to insist that punishment cannot be viewed in purely consequentialist or utilitarian terms. They have felt that there is a moral element to punishment which we do not do justice to if we justify it purely by talking of its beneficial results for the individual or even his society as a whole.

I agree that punishment is not to be justified exclusively by its consequences, and in general my view of ethics is far from consequentialist or utilitarian. In saying that the general aim of punishment is deterrence I have not appealed only to its consequences to justify the institution of punishment, for I have repeatedly emphasized that we are justified in deterring offenders through *punishment*, rather than other means, because punishment, properly understood, respects the individual's capacity for choice and his responsibility for directing his own life. Then too punishment, by characteristically falling on offenders and not on the innocent, is in harmony with our moral sense of what is just and fitting. I have certainly spelled out some of the *advantages* of this, in terms of security and confidence for example, partly in order to de-mystify notions such as 'responsibility', but the point is not simply that being allowed to take responsibility for your own life, through the institution of punishment, tends to have a pleasant outcome rather than the reverse (for this might equally be brought about by other means). Rather, the nature of the value of such responsibility is revealed, as I shall try to show in a later chapter, by its connection with other moral values such as freedom and the capacity to consider reasons.

To talk of deterrence in answering *one* sort of question about the justification of punishment does not imply a general justification of punishment in purely consequential terms. The supposition that it does mean this simply shows how easily various *different* questions about the justification of punishment can become confused and treated as one.

7

Punishment and the Moral Order

One way of expressing a central argument of the last chapter is to say that punishment is related to morality (or ethical considerations, or the moral life, or the moral order of things) in a way that many other means of achieving order are not. Responsibility and choice, which punishment respects, are linked to the notions of right and wrong which lie at the heart of morality. For it would make no sense to commend a person for doing right, or blame him for doing wrong, if he had no choice in the matter or could not properly be said to be responsible. A pupil is not blameworthy for an involuntary (and unexaggerated) fit of coughing, however much it disrupts the lesson, since he did not choose to be seized by it. (He might of course be to blame for coming to school in that state, or his parents might be to blame for letting or making him come.)

The unease which talk of morality sometimes provokes is such that a degree of reassurance may be helpful here. In talking of 'the moral order' I do not mean to convey that I think there is some fixed, unvarying array of commands and prohibitions that we all have to obey. Rather the phrase indicates the moral dimension to life, the range of considerations about what we ought to do, what is for the best and what sort of life we ought to live, that human beings can escape from only by resigning their powers of deliberation and choice and becoming automata. To talk of moral issues is not necessarily to insist that we ought to do this or that, or that people should live their lives in any particular way. But it is to insist that ideas of duty, of what ought to be done, of right and wrong, justice, fairness and other virtues, simply could not be eliminated from the thought and practice of creatures recognizably like ourselves.

The purpose of this chapter is to investigate two aspects in particular of the relationship between punishment and morality: the

71

claim that punishment brings about moral learning, and the role of retribution. First, however, it may make for greater clarity if I emphasize that my argument so far has been about the general practice of punishment or, as it is sometimes put, the *institution* of punishment. That a society or community employs the institution of punishment means that it characteristically attempts to secure order by punishment as I have defined it rather than by pre-emptive psychological treatment, periodic purges of 'unreliable elements' or simple bullying. It is the wholesale replacement of punishment by these other kinds of practice that I have suggested would be morally objectionable. Such a society, or one where we found something similar to the institution of punishment but less carefully operated (perhaps they did not worry overmuch if penalties often fell on the innocent) would be a morally thinner place. Its members would have less responsibility for their own lives, less security in the future. This, then, is the sense in which my argument relates punishment to morality: the *institution* of punishment is morally more satisfactory than the alternatives. It does not of course follow from this that on any particular occasion punishment is automatically the morally appropriate response, that we are morally obliged invariably to punish offenders rather than, say, forgive them or remind them of the rules (and perhaps the reasons for the rules) that they have broken. This conclusion would require one of those more extreme theses, to the effect either that punishment is an important source of moral learning, or that retribution is good in itself, that I shall now examine.

I shall criticize first P. S. Wilson's attempts (1971 and 1974) to connect punishment with morality and with moral learning not because the case he makes out is an especially weak one but, on the contrary, because it is sophisticated and has proved influential. Wilson holds that we can properly speak of punishment only where breaches of specifically *moral* rules are in question. Where a person is made to pay simply for stepping outside limits laid down for the smooth running of an institution or society he is not, properly speaking, 'punished', Wilson believes, but penalized. Being penalized is just a matter of making a payment or suffering a disadvantage for breaking rules, while punishment is 'a matter of learning that breaking rules which one values *oneself* is not just something for which, if caught, one must pay, but something which, whether one is caught at it or not, is "wrong" and therefore, morally speaking, deserves to fail' (1971, p. 98). I penalize a pupil, then, for disrupting a lesson by talking at the back of the class, but I punish the child who wishes to learn my subject, agrees to do the homework but, through weakness of will perhaps, fails to do so. (These are my examples, not Wilson's.) Although probably few teachers make this distinction consciously I think that one of the conclusions Wilson draws will find an echo in many:

> Punishment, to me, is something educative. In it is revealed an entirely different dimension of value (namely, the moral dimension), from that which is bounded merely by fear of loss and hope of gain. (1971, p. 112)

> Punishment, I have suggested, is part of our education. It helps to initiate us . . . into the moral dimension of life. (ibid., p. 117)

It is of some importance whether Wilson is right or not, for his argument seems to confer legitimacy on the view, widespread among teachers and others, that punishment may have a positively beneficial effect on the individual punished.

P. S. Wilson wants to ensure that punishment is something more than just a reflection of the will of the teacher, that it is not simply a device for making people do whatever the punisher happens to want them to do. So he ties punishment to specifically moral rules, which are independent of the will of particular persons. He also wants to argue that punishment brings about moral learning. There are two distinct claims here. One is a legitimate philosophical claim to the effect that it would make sense, or fit in with our best intuitions about the world, to regard punishment in the way Wilson describes. The other looks more like an empirical claim about what would as a matter of fact happen if we took this view of punishment. It will therefore require empirical evidence to support it, for it certainly is not guaranteed by a teacher's belief that he is punishing for the breach of a specifically moral rule that the pupil will come to see the rule in the same light. It is as always possible that he will interpret the teacher's action as mere revenge or simple injustice. Empirical evidence aside, however, we can still consider the coherence and plausibility of the second claim.

Reserving punishment for infringements of moral rules or for things that are 'wrong' rather than inconvenient would require us to be able to make a sufficiently clear distinction between moral rules and other ones, and between the action of punishing and that of penalizing. I have already (above, p. 67) cast doubt on the coherence of the distinction between punishments and penalties. It seems to me that there is a moral dimension to behaviour which Wilson would penalize rather than punish: parking on double yellow lines or running down the corridors are acts of selfishness or disregard for others. This begins to make the distinction look blurred. And what are the characteristics of a *punishment*, according to Wilson, by which a person may know he is being punished rather than merely penalized? We might expect a punishment, being for a breach of moral rules, to involve the offender being made to feel guilty or ashamed. That is exactly what we find in Wilson's clearest example of what a punishment looks like. A girl has failed to practise a piano piece adequately: at her next lesson her teacher rattles loose coins in his pocket, 'gets up and begins pacing up and down behind her back in a caged sort of way . . . looks out of the window, goes across to the bookcase, takes out a book and starts reading it; worst of all . . . throughout all this he heaves deep sighs from time to time' (1974, p. 107). This falls within the moral area, Wilson thinks, because the girl promised or agreed to practise the piano. So her teacher's behaviour communicates to her that she deserves as a moral agent to suffer the sort of displeasure with herself (pp. 126–7) that looks very much like guilt or shame, though Wilson does not use these words.

The trouble is that the range of actions for which we can and do make people feel guilty is vast. As I pointed out above, in this sense of punishment a great deal of 'punishing' goes on in human relationships. If someone close to me annoys me or has plans of their own which conflict with mine I can easily withdraw my love or approval and so cause them to feel rotten, guilty or obscurely displeased with themselves. There are some people who are quite capable of making one feel guilty for almost anything and everything, who radiate a kind of disapproval that suggests no one can quite come up to their exacting standards. A sensible scheme of things, I suggest, will make as sharp a distinction as possible between punishment and moral blackmail. Making people feel guilty is not a distinguishing mark of punishment. We can even turn wide areas of actions into *moral* failings by exacting solemn promises and then displaying shock at others' failure to keep them. In this way Wilson's music teacher appears to have turned what one might have thought was the morally insignificant business of not practising the piano into an occasion for hours of rumination and self-recrimination (ibid., p. 107) by getting his pupil to make a promise. (No wonder the poor girl doesn't practise the piano: the adults around her are making it very clear that playing the piano is worth very little when compared with brooding on one's minor weaknesses of will.) My own memories of school are full of incidents of this sort: when teachers, leaving the classroom for a few minutes, would extract such solemn promises, or 'put us on our honour', to behave. Then they could later generate an atmosphere heavy with guilt and shame by lecturing us on how we had let ourselves down.

On the analysis of punishment that I favour it is of course perfectly possible for adults and teachers to punish children for absurd things. The rules we lay down can be trivial, self-contradictory or plain foolish. That is why it is so important that on this conception of punishment there are safeguards for offenders: they are at least to know the rules in advance and will have a pretty good idea of what they are likely to suffer from breaking them. Anyone disinclined to accept that some of the rules of his own society or institution may conceivably be foolish has only to look elsewhere, historically or geographically: rules forbidding the teaching of evolution in some parts of the USA until recently, forbidding mixed marriages in South Africa, forbidding freedom of speech in the Soviet Union. Where there is punishment, as I have defined it, for these offences at least it can be anticipated and avoided by those who want to. Furthermore, where you are punished, properly speaking, it is only your behaviour that is penalized: you can go on valuing what the state discounts and thinking what you like. Your mind is still free. Then too punishment comes to an end: the penalty is paid and the business is over. Where we set out to make people feel guilty, however, there is less possibility of anticipation. In fact, as I spell out below, if we think we are thus educating them morally we are likely to make them feel guilty for things they did not perceive as involving guilt and where therefore anticipation is impossible. To instil guilt is to colour the mind, not just to influence behaviour, and guilt has no limit or end in the way that punishment does. My point can be summed up by saying that it is true enough that we often punish people misguidedly and for the wrong things, but heaven forbid we move to a conception of punishment that we imagine justifies us in making people feel guilty. For when we cause people to feel guilty the damage we may do is much greater.

There is also a logical oddity in supposing that it is the business of punishment to bring about moral learning. This implies that the offender did not know that what he did was wrong. After all, it is in order to teach him the wrongness that, allegedly, he is being punished. But how can we punish someone who did not know he was doing wrong? At the very least it is strange to turn to punishment as a first resort in such cases: normally we would start with explanation and warning. In any case, we tend to think that motive and intention are of some importance in determining what offence, if any, has been committed, but a person who did not know he was doing wrong has not offended intentionally at all. On the other hand, if the offender knows he has done wrong, what (on this view of punishment) is the point of punishing him? Punishment only reveals the moral order if

75

the offender is ready to see it as punishment, that is as something connected to morality rather than revenge, reprisal or what P. S. Wilson would call a 'penalty'. But if he sees it as a punishment he must already grasp the moral order and so the punishment appears superfluous. According to Wilson (1971, p. 118), 'the *force* of what we say or do in punishing hurts, while the *meaning* educates' (his italics). What is the connection between force and meaning here? If we are ready to perceive the meaning, what is the point of the force? It is gratuitous if the only aim of punishment is to educate morally.

Sometimes the slightly weaker claim is made that punishment *confirms* the moral order, reassuring the child that his growing intuitions about right and wrong are correct and conferring the security that comes from living in a morally regular world. If this means that punishments must clearly be fair, falling on the guilty rather than the innocent and being roughly in proportion to offences, I would not disagree. No doubt it is confusing and disturbing for a child to witness or suffer excessive punishment or victimization. Often, however, something more is meant: perhaps that a child who, say, copies another's work out of weakness of will, while appearing to know well enough that cheating is wrong, will have his knowledge ratified and his will strengthened by punishment. Or perhaps the idea is that when he sees another child punished for doing something that he was fairly sure was wrong his grasp of the moral issues is corroborated and becomes more certain. In both cases what is going on can either be interpreted as effectively deterrence or seen as a kind of teaching, but either way I think there are serious problems if punishment is linked specifically to infringements of the moral order.

For we need to consider rather more deeply what we mean by 'the moral order'. As I said at the beginning of this chapter, the moral dimension of our lives does not consist in a clear and unalterable list of injunctions and prohibitions. First, there is room for argument and disagreement about what is morally of most importance: cheating is to be deplored, but so is smugly turning a deaf ear to a friend's appeal for help. I happen to find it very objectionable (and I am prepared to justify calling this a moral matter) to stereotype people as typical feminists, socialists or whatever, yet I find some people whose opinion I generally respect place this very low in their list of moral priorities. Secondly, it is often very difficult to determine whether a particular action falls under a certain description even when you are clear that actions that do so fall are deplorable: bullying is deplorable, but what looks like bullying to me may strike you as teasing and some of the children involved may genuinely think they are just 'having a bit of fun'. Thirdly, to adopt a distinction of Hart's (1969, pp. 71 ff.), morality involves not just certain material values which may change with place and time, as our society generally now tolerates homosexuality, which at other times has been illegal, but also what he calls 'formal values' which are essential to having any kind of morality at all: impartiality, say, and a degree of readiness to take account of the values and preferences of others.

Morality, in short, is a complex and subtle area. The idea that punishment confirms or teaches the moral order or is an appropriate deterrent only where specifically moral wrongs are in question is plausible only with a drastically simplified view which reduces morality to a clear-cut set of rules. Punishment cannot teach the underlying principles. It cannot show just what it is in virtue of which we call this fruitful co-operation but that cheating, why this counts as teasing but that counts as bullying. Indeed if punishment in the name of moral education is likely to teach children anything it is that the spirit of concern for others or the passion for justice, which are at the root of much of our moral thinking, are of negligible importance beside the careful observance of the prevailing code. In the terms of P. S. Wilson's example, anxiety to keep to the letter of the moral law consigns to oblivion the love of music without which the whole exercise loses its point.

Perhaps children, up to adolescence at least, prefer a morally rigid, codified environment and feel safer in it. But the real world is not like this: it is a place of moral conflicts, uncertainties and grey areas. An education in morality must acknowledge this complexity and not be satisfied with what can be most easily taught, what children will most readily accept or what is administratively most convenient. It is strange that on the one hand we like to think school rewards and punishments initiate children into the wider world of moral considerations while on the other schools' rules and values often seem part of nothing more than a bizarre, self-contained game. An extreme example: I was once with a senior teacher while he berated an adult-looking girl of about fifteen for failing to wear her uniform properly. She was, he told her, letting down both herself and the school. Clearly he felt there were moral issues at stake: 'You ought to be ashamed of yourself'. Later he confided to me that this was a difficult pupil, known to be working as a prostitute during weekends and her frequent truancies. It was hard not to see the girl's blank indifference to the fuss about uniform as a reasonable response to its true significance in her life as a whole.

If we wish to help children to a better understanding of the moral dimension, of why some things are right and others are wrong, to put it at its simplest, I suggest we have to take seriously the idea that in this area as in others the teacher has to explain and give reasons. Bringing home to somebody the wrongness of a course of action is not a causal process, a matter of making them feel guilty. We can make people feel guilty without their understanding why. This is hardly moral learning. Once we accept the importance of giving reasons here punishment begins to look an inadequate way to teach moral lessons, for it conveys no reasons or explanations. Not even the view that punishment exists to convey the brute fact *that* certain things are wrong entails that it is a particularly suitable way of doing so. As Hart (1969, p. 66) writes, 'The normal way in which moral condemnation is expressed is by *words*, and it is not clear, if denunciation is really what is required, why a solemn public statement of disapproval would not be the most "appropriate" or "emphatic" means of expressing this.'

This brings me to the last topic of this chapter, that of retribution, for there is a connection between retribution and the giving of reasons that I shall come to presently. First however it is necessary to make a distinction between retribution in distribution, as Hart puts it, and retribution as general justifying aim. To hold that punishment is or must be in its nature retributive may be no more than to insist that punishment may be inflicted only on offenders and not on the innocent. This is retribution in distribution, and in this sense most people's view of punishment is retributive. In fact it is possible to claim that this is part of the meaning of punishment and that measures which do not include at least this element of retribution really cannot be called punishment at all.

Some however go considerably further than this and maintain that where a person has done wrong and caused pain or suffering it is right and proper that suffering should be inflicted on him in return: 'Wicked conduct injuring others itself calls for punishment, and calls for it even if its infliction is not necessary in order to prevent repetition of that conduct by the offender or by others' (Hart, 1968, p. 234). That is, they hold that punishment of the guilty is a kind of intrinsic good quite apart from any deterrent or even reformative effects it may happen to have. They may go so far as to insist that there is an obligation on us to punish offenders: an extreme version of this is expressed by Kant, who in an often-quoted passage in the *Philosophy of Law* (trans. Hastie, 1887) wrote that a society on the verge of dissolution (we might think of this as the brief space between warning of nuclear attack and annihilation) has the duty to execute the last murderer left in its gaols before the end. Perhaps this is just Kant's way of dramatizing his philosophical conviction that the moral value of punishment, as of other moral goods, does not consist in its having any beneficial *consequences*, for in the circumstances he describes there can of course be none. We should respect the difficulty that the retributivist of this sort finds himself in, for any reasons he gives for the good of punishment may suggest he in fact values punishment for something else, for what the reasons point to, and that is incompatible with punishment being an *intrinsic* good. Still, those of us who find the notion of the intrinsic goodness of punishment repugnant or baffling may fairly require the idea to be made clearer to us. For why should we take seriously a claim for which no justification is offered?

One line of defence is that it is unjust that a wrongdoer should prosper while his victims or others suffer – that the petty thief should enjoy the satisfaction of having eaten the sweets while those he has robbed are the poorer. Here retribution is closely related to two other ideas: those of compensation and of giving satisfaction to or assuaging the feelings of the aggrieved or injured. But we must distinguish reparation from retaliation. It is one thing, when a child deliberately spoils another's belongings, to make him exchange his own book for the one spoiled or pay for a replacement (no doubt with some indication that that was a mean or unkind thing to do). It is quite another for the teacher to spoil the child's own book in return. This may well appeal to a basic or primitive sense of justice, not least because the punishment seems so neatly to fit the offence, but it is precisely what weight we should give this desire for justice that is in question, especially in the face of the obvious fact that tit-for-tat adds to the sum of misery in the world. Not all our intuitions about the moral order, not even those which like the urge for justice appear unadulterated by non-moral considerations, are necessarily to be followed. In the balance against the kind of retribution I am discussing here stand not only factors which some would call non-moral, such as what *good* retribution does, but also other specifically moral motives such as mercy and patience. It seems unjust that the wrongdoer should prosper, but where there is no hope of compensation to the injured and where deterrence or teaching the wrongness of the offence are not at issue we must take seriously the possibility that simple retribution is more of an evil than a good.

In any case there is no question of compensation for many sorts of offence, especially in schools. For who is compensated when, for example, a pupil is put into detention for being late and missing morning assembly? As far as the teachers are concerned the punishment, like most school punishments, is a further inconvenience rather than a compensation. I must emphasize that my remarks here apply only to the justification of punishment on retributive grounds and not to punishment as a deterrent. It is the idea that punishment is all the more justified because the pupil 'mustn't be allowed to get away with it' that needs to be challenged. Do the feelings of the injured and the aggrieved deserve to be assuaged? These feelings are to the effect that the offender ought to suffer for what he has done, and are to be acted upon only if we can find independent grounds for thinking that he so ought. They do not in themselves give us a reason for retribution, any more than the offender's feeling that he should go scot-free is itself a reason for letting him go.

It is obvious enough that a teacher should not get into the habit of thinking that he is justified in punishing a pupil to the extent that it satisfies his feelings of resentment. When your lesson is disrupted or your instructions are ignored it is natural to be angry and the infringement of rule or routine may warrant a punishment for deterrent purposes, but the anger is not the reason for the punishment – it does not *justify* it – and had better not appear to be the reason. To take the line 'You've hurt me and now I'm going to hurt you' may conceivably bring a degree of satisfaction, varying from individual to individual, but is not thereby guaranteed as justice. Most of us have powerful intuitions about justice and injustice but our feelings are not an infallible guide to what is just in particular situations, especially when we are personally involved in the role of authority and our fragile self-esteem is at risk. What feels to me like justified resentment may to you look much more like a mixture of fear, insecurity and frustration. I part company entirely with those such as P. S. Wilson who believe it is beneficial for there to be a personal element in punishment on the grounds that this may repair the estrangement and alienation which, in schools, is likely to have been at the root of misbehaviour in the first place. There is such a wealth of evidence (such as Corrigan's, 1979) that pupils are only too ready to find personal elements in school punishments, regarding retribution for mischief as being motivated purely by the teacher's spite or desire for revenge. Where this happens a pupil may feel himself quite justified in further retaliation against the teacher, and the result is the familiar cycle of mutual recrimination. The better teachers I have known have not made their pupils feel that their misdemeanours consisted in their upsetting *them*, any more than they conveyed the message that the distinctive quality of good work was its bringing pleasure to the teacher. Their own sense of security, I think, was strong enough for them not to need to do that. Here is a further advantage of tying punishment to the breach of rules: it reduces the element of personal confrontation. If we wish to improve personal relationships between teachers and taught this is one way to begin, and there are better ways of continuing than through punishments.

Those writers impressed by the moral dimension of punishment have often leant towards a retributive view of the general justifying aim. In part this is because, as I sketched above (p. 55ff), the way reasons enter into morality is far from simple. To give reasons for moral judgements can look suspiciously like appealing to non-moral considerations. This viewpoint owes much to Kant, who wrote that a 'good will', or specifically moral motive, 'is not good because of what it effects or accomplishes' (*Groundwork*, ed. Paton, 1976, para. 3): an action that has genuinely moral worth is not motivated by the thought that it is a means to some further end such as one's own or others' happiness, welfare or honour. That would mean the action was based on what Kant called 'empirical' principles, which 'are always unfitted to serve as a ground for moral laws' (ibid., para. 90). Moral laws should hold for all human beings and not just those who happen to have various inclinations, towards maximizing others' well-being or anything else. It is easy to see how close this is to claiming that an action with moral worth is not done for any sort of *reason*. Thus in justifying punishment there has been a reluctance amongst some to talk in terms of deterrent or other effects which would constitute the *reason* for punishing, and a preference for claiming that the good of punishment simply consists in the plain fact that it inflicts suffering or inconvenience on the offender in return for the suffering or inconvenience he has caused. On similar grounds perhaps there has been a temptation to suppose that explanation is a flawed means of moral education: that giving children reasons why some things are right and others wrong comes perilously close to appealing to non-moral factors. Then it would be natural to look to the simple experience of punishment to bring about changes in moral thinking, and to hold, as John Wilson does (1983, p. 524), that 'Retribution is in effect partly an educational device, designed to achieve a particular kind of understanding'.

I have already tried to show how taking deterrent effects as the general justifying aim of punishment need not detract from punishment's having a specifically moral dimension which is not shared by certain alternative means of achieving order. I have also suggested that explaining can take many forms other than the explicit giving of reasons. We can appeal to the imagination of the child ('How would you like it if . . .?'), construct parables and allegories, use works of literature and films to enrich someone's conception of a quality such as pride or of a particular way of life.

Thus we may be able to help children look quite deeply into why some ways of behaving are morally objectionable and others are to be emulated, more so than if we simply relied on retribution to teach them that doing harm to others is usually followed by come-uppance – the only lesson that retribution on its own can possibly teach. In any case what children need to learn about justice is not that it characteristically metes out measure for measure. Their vision of the world tends readily to encompass that idea of justice, as a few minutes' observation of children at play is likely to confirm. What children (and not only children) are less quick to grasp is that justice may involve other, more subtle factors such as the evaluation of intention and that justice itself is only one element, albeit an important one, in the moral life. Emphasis on retribution will hardly help children to appreciate these factors and give them their proper weight: it may even hinder them.

There is one more argument in support of retribution that I want to consider finally because it raises both directly and in passing important educational issues. Some offenders, it is sometimes said, feel a positive need for punishment and may actually welcome it, in order to expiate their wrongdoing and 'wipe the slate clean'. The classic case of this, and one often cited in support of retributive doctrines, is that of Raskolnikov, in Dostoyevsky's novel *Crime and Punishment*. Raskolnikov murders an old woman, a miserly money-lender, not for the sake of personal gain but believing the world will be well rid of her and intending to distribute her money to the poor. After the murder he gradually has a change of heart. Eventually he admits his crime to the authorities and is sent to prison in Siberia, where he is followed by the devoted Sonia. There he first regards his situation with sullen indifference but after some time he undergoes a transformation and comes to accept his imprisonment willingly: he feels sufficient remorse for his crime to want to atone for it by suffering punishment. There are still seven years of his sentence to run: 'What great suffering and what infinite joy till then! And he had come back to life, and he knew it, and felt it with every fibre of his renewed being' (Penguin translation, 1982, p. 558).

The first thing to notice is that Raskolnikov's case runs counter to many common ideas about retribution and punishment. For punishment does not cause him to feel remorse or repentance: on the contrary, it is his repentance that brings him to accept his imprisonment as proper punishment for what he has done. This may seem puzzling. What is the *good* to Raskolnikov of suffering retribution, since he already acknowledges the wrongfulness of his crime? Unless it quenches some masochistic thirst for humiliation, what satisfaction or benefit can legal punishment bring a man who fully accepts his guilt? It is hard to answer these questions explicitly. Yet Dostoyevsky's story has by many readers been felt to be not merely plausible but profoundly true. This is a second point of importance. Here we have an example of the way our moral understanding may be enriched, of how we may be morally educated, without having spelled out to us a series of clauses beginning 'because'. If *Crime and Punishment* is plausible we shall have to take more seriously the possibility that under certain circumstances retribution may be a good to the offender, even though it is difficult to give a clear account of the reasons why it is such a good. In this way novels, like plays and films and other works of art, can *show* truths that can hardly be stated explicitly. Novels, as one philosopher who has written about Raskolnikov's case puts it, enable us

> to imagine just what it would be like to be a particular individual in a particular moral crisis (however uncommon or extraordinary) and, through their power to bring alive these moral predicaments, exhibit the attractiveness or otherwise of particular moral solutions . . . when one reads depictions as vivid and detailed as those of Raskolnikov's acceptance of imprisonment, when his moral need for punishment is brought so compellingly before us, the notion of a right to punishment ceases to seem absurd and begins to become morally plausible. (Sophie Botros, 1983)

Still, *Crime and Punishment*, however plausible, is not the last word on the subject. We might in the end decide that it was just 'part of Dostoyevsky's private world, described with such power that one momentarily took it to be how the real world is' (Glover, 1970). However (and this is the third point of importance) to the extent that *Crime and Punishment* is convincing it suggests the limitations of accounts of punishment which emphasize the benefits for communities and institutions at the expense of what Sophie Botros (1983) calls the 'private conscience' or 'moral self' and its inner claims. Thus Dostoyevsky's novel is deeply anti-utilitarian in tendency and may appear a valuable corrective to theories of punishment in which deterrence is regarded as the general justifying aim, however carefully that position is qualified as I have tried to do with my own account. How far, then, can we accept Dostoyevsky's picture and generalize from it?

Obviously I am not attempting here to do full justice to the central theme of a complex novel: I confine myself to only a few remarks. I think it is essential to appreciate that Raskolnikov's is a special and unusual case. When he commits the crime he regards the old woman as 'vermin' and explicitly sees himself as a different species of person, one of a breed of extraordinary men who are above the law. For such a person, experiencing a change of heart will involve coming to think of himself as within the law once again, and repentance will naturally be accompanied by the need or desire to suffer legal punishment. For to repent of seeing yourself as above the law just is to accept the law's penalties where they are appropriate: repentance here cannot be separated from being subject to judicial punishment as it ordinarily can. In so far then as Raskolnikov is described as feeling a positive longing for punishment and standing to benefit by accepting suffering and being redeemed by it (the narrative can be interpreted differently), it is possible for us to find *Crime and Punishment* plausible without endorsing any kind of general thesis about the intrinsic good of retribution. Those who, like Raskolnikov, consciously and avowedly put themselves above the law are probably rare. They are seldom likely to include schoolchildren.

Certainly children sometimes misbehave so blatantly and repeatedly that we are tempted to conclude they really want to be punished. But we need to treat such cases cautiously. The child may be seeking the approval of its peers: perhaps showing contempt to authority and indifference to its punishments will bring prestige and a reputation for being tough. Or there are occasions when a person may seek punishment in order to rid himself of feelings of guilt and 'wipe the slate clean' with no better motive than to be able to re-offend with a clear conscience. Then too it is sometimes reasonable to regard blatant misbehaviour as a 'cry for attention' on the part of a child incoherently trying to communicate distress of some sort. Some teachers who pride themselves on hard-headed realism dismiss such ideas as 'liberal permissiveness' or like to reply grimly that if it's attention they want it's attention they are going to get. But there do exist such children as the pupil of mine whose father I discovered to have died after lengthy illness on the very morning I was contemplating how to punish the boy for his repeated interruptions and other infractions. It is not always at all easy to find which of the children laying claim to our attention in unacceptable ways have reasons, as in this case, with which we would sympathize. The possibility of making a cruel mistake should suggest a large degree of caution to even the most hard-headed. Perhaps any attention, even that of being punished, is welcome to a chronically unhappy or neglected child. Yet as we saw with moral education, so with attention: there are better ways of supplying it than through punishment.

I do not think we should be very impressed, then, by the claim that wrongdoers in general or even any very large class of them crave retribution and are positively benefited by it. Anyone still inclined to be so impressed ought certainly to read *Crime and Punishment* carefully and consider, among other matters, what role in Raskolnikov's slow change of heart is played by the patient unwavering love of his companion, Sonia. If Dostoyevsky has a lesson for us it is not about the ready benefits of brisk retribution.

8

Justice and Other Virtues

The conclusion I have reached about the general justifying aim of punishment seems to invite misunderstandings. It tends to be widely assumed, first, that a defender of a deterrence theory ought in consistency to be prepared to punish the innocent. For this might prove an exceptionally powerful deterrent, partly because it would suggest perhaps that real offenders would be punished all the more severely if even those who had done nothing wrong suffered penalties. On these grounds it is often concluded that deterrence is impossible as a general aim. That this is not so however should be clear from my insistence throughout that punishment is an institution with built-in safeguards: the innocent are not to be punished, excuses and extenuating circumstances are to be taken into consideration, and so on. This particular misunderstanding might arise less readily if the theory I have defended was labelled as one of *qualified* deterrence. That is, the general aim of punishment is to deter within the limits of the safeguards I have described.

Secondly, talk of deterrence suggests to some that severe, not to say savage, measures would be justified, as being most likely to deter. And so again they conclude that no civilized community should employ deterrent punishment. Here it is necessary to recall the further qualification that punishment must be economical, both in the sense that no punishment should cause more distress than the offence would have if left unchecked, and in the sense that a severer punishment should not be employed if a more lenient one would have the same deterrent effect. Precise calculation, whether of amount of distress or of deterrent capacity, is obviously impossible here. But this qualification is enough to show in general terms that a deterrent view of punishment does not license brutality. It may be, too, that in many cases the mere fact that a teacher *notices* misbehaviour sufficiently to punish it is enough to deter further mischief. There is empirical evidence, to which I return below, that in classrooms pinpointing offenders in good time is more important than the kind of sanction, if any, used against them.

There is therefore absolutely no reason to assume, as I find people very ready to, that a proponent of a deterrent theory of punishment is automatically a supporter of corporal punishment. The assumption is made, I suppose, largely because beating is so often called a school's 'ultimate deterrent'. But the existence of such slogans no more commits anyone who takes the view of punishment that I do to beating children than slogans about 'nuclear deterrence' in themselves commit anyone who wishes to avoid war to supporting the maintenance of nuclear weapons. In both cases the important questions are whether these things really do deter and do so economically. It is possible to argue that corporal punishment does not in fact deter children from wrongdoing (school punishment books tend to record the same children being beaten regularly); as always there really is no way of telling whether those who behave well do so because they are deterred. In any case it can also be argued that corporal punishment inflicts too great a degree of suffering, in the form less of pain than of humiliation, for its use to be acceptable, whatever the deterrent effects. Thus it falls to the qualification that punishment must be economical in the sense I have outlined. There is evidence too that beating children, especially in front of others, has unpleasant effects on those innocent ones who are compelled either to witness it or even to know it is taking place. Fear of pain and humiliation become transmuted, by a psychological defence mechanism, into fascination with them (cf. Docking, 1980, p. 232, and the studies cited there). Moreover if what I have written about retribution is correct teachers ought to abandon the idea that beating is an especially suitable response to certain kinds of delinquency such as bullying on the grounds that it 'fits the crime'. This is either the crudest, eye-for-an-eye kind of retributivism or it conceals the belief that the bully will learn from being hurt that hurting people is wrong. This claim requires empirical backing which does not appear to exist. It is at least equally likely that the bully will conclude that it is perfectly acceptable to bully as long as you are in a position of authority.

Deprived of the sanction of corporal punishment, many teachers feel that they are left with few effective deterrents. Detentions, impositions, putting a pupil 'on report', setting tasks of tidying and cleaning represent the typical punishments at a teacher's regular disposal. It will be said that they are certainly not going to deter the aggressive adolescent who hates school and is hell-bent on turning every encounter with a teacher into a confrontation. However I do

87

not think that is what we should expect of the kinds of punishment available to teachers. They are not meant to inspire sufficient terror to cow the die-hards: if they did that they would have to be so extreme as to keep the ordinary child forever looking nervously over his shoulder, and I do not think that is what we want. All we can ask of school punishments is that they give pause to children who are thinking of doing what they know is forbidden and make more ready to think those who for one reason or another are not inclined to. A deterrent is no *guarantee* of compliance, and ought not to be.

There are three responses that we can make to the fact that school punishments are not enormously effective as deterrents. First, we can try to dream up more stringent sanctions in the hope that they will prove more effective. But even if they do they may not be economical in the sense I have outlined. In any case this raises a general point about the way in which we formulate our philosophy of punishment. It is a fundamental mistake, I believe, to do so in such a way as to put maximum power into the hands of those in authority. Some of them, perhaps most, will punish wisely and justly, but it is necessary also to protect those liable to be on the receiving end of punishment from people in authority who punish foolishly, spitefully or without sufficient forethought. (Teachers anxious for solutions to pressing practical problems are only too likely to fall under this category.) Punishment is not to be seen solely from the point of view of the righteous in their crusade, moral or otherwise, against the forces of evil. Our arrangements concerning punishment must be such as to protect the punished from suffering excessively, undeservedly or both. In this respect formulating a philosophy of punishment is rather like designing a car. You can do so with the sole or principal aim of giving the driver the greatest possible amount of power and speed, and hope (or assume) that he will drive sensibly. Or you can design it so as to minimize the damage it can do, both to the environment generally and to other road-users, if it is misused.

Secondly, we can take the practice of punishment in schools as it exists as given and look for some other role for it to play. That is, realizing that our punishments are not very powerful as deterrents but unable to imagine teaching without them we can come to think of them as something else: as instruments of moral education, for example. I have been concerned throughout the last couple of chapters to counter this move, which has commonly been made during the last twenty or so years as thinking about punishment has supposedly become more liberal and civilized. Punishment may not be as useful as a deterrent as we once imagined, but it is quite out of place in the other roles for which it has been cast.

The third possible response, of course, is simply to give up punishing where the deterrent effects do not justify it.

To do this is not to give up hope of making schools and classrooms fitter places for learning to go on in, though some no doubt will find it hard to accept this. There are other ways of doing some of the things which I have argued punishment does so badly. For a start, if we want children to learn a sense of justice perhaps they will do so through exploring imaginatively what it is like to be another person, thus gaining insight into what it really means to be treated in ways one would find intolerable oneself. Education offers all sorts of opportunities for this sort of exploration. It may be, too, that children learn justice and fairness simply by being treated justly and fairly, and there are other ways of doing this than by ensuring they pay the full price for all their misdemeanours. This is partly a question of what is involved in having a sense of justice, of course, and partly an empirical question of how whatever qualities we decide make up the just individual can be acquired. It is not altogether obvious, even, that if we want to bring children up to be better people and live morally more satisfactory and satisfying lives, then it is first and foremost justice and related virtues that should be at the front of their moral consciousnesses. 'Between friends there is no need of justice', Aristotle wrote (*Nicomachean Ethics*, Bk. 8, ch. 1), and similarly Hume felt that justice was made redundant by extensive benevolence – not a common phenomenon, admittedly, 'but still we may observe, that the case of families approaches towards it; and the stronger the mutual benevolence is among the individuals, the nearer it approaches' (*Enquiries*, para. 146). This contrasts vividly with John Wilson's view (above, p. 46), of the family as a quasi-military institution where discipline is of the first importance. My point here is not the trite one that all would be well if only people were more well-disposed towards each other. Rather it is that there is room for real disagreement over what qualities we want to characterize our institutions and the people in them. Not only, then, are there better ways of teaching children justice than simply subjecting them to it in its retributive form: perhaps a well-ordered school or community might be one where justice was not regarded as the chief of the virtues at all; where the words used to describe how a person ought to live came primarily not from the (Kantian) tradition where the crucial notions are those of justice, equality and desert but from rather different ethical traditions in which the notions of benevolence, sympathy or even love play a central role.

School punishments are poor deterrents: I have argued too that they are bad at communicating reasons, at making clear to a child the nature of his wrongdoing. I suggested that retributivists tend to view this limitation with equanimity since they are inclined to undervalue the place of reason-giving in the moral life. Once we have reinstated reasons, however, we can conceive it as part of our job as teachers to explain or show how and why certain actions are wrong, selfish, inconsiderate or whatever. This will often require us to engage with particular children and try to understand why it is that the individual before us has trouble in perceiving the nature of his or her behaviour: why does *this* girl appear not to realize she is being intolerably rude? What does *she* think she is doing? It is extra-ordinary but true that just as there is a folk-wisdom in the teaching profession about the dangers of being too friendly with pupils and of forming genuinely personal relationships with them, so too there is a tendency to depreciate communication and discussion. For example, P. Francis (1975, p. 134) declares firmly 'Do not discuss a crisis situation with a class'. One large north-eastern comprehensive includes in its information to new and student teachers this advice under the heading 'Sanctions': 'If a pupil persistently disrupts a lesson you . . . should in extreme cases consult the classteacher, Head of Department, Head of House, Deputy Heads', thus conveying the impression that communication between teachers about professional problems is something which will take place only in the last resort. Yet it might be supposed that high among the qualities of a good teacher are the ability and willingness to communicate with colleagues and superiors as well as with whole classes and individual children. How else do we ever learn anything?

In order to communicate effectively with individual pupils we need to see them as individuals. This is not easy. At the best of times we find ourselves regarding other people as the occupants of roles, as typical teachers, policemen and so on. In schools children come to us most of the time in large groups ready-labelled as third-formers, 'remedials', 'a difficult class'. When watching someone else teaching a class it is often obvious how little chance the harassed teacher, his attention largely on the material he is trying to put across, has really to listen to or properly notice the individual children and what they are doing and saying. No wonder they frequently appear to offend and disobey almost as if they wanted to be caught doing so, as a kind of claim on our attention. Again I think we must consider the possibility that there are better ways of giving children the attention they seek than through punishment. It is interesting how many studies of classrooms stress the importance of the teacher *noticing* everything that is going on, of his displaying what Kounin (1970) calls 'withitness': this appears to matter more than any action he takes or how angry or firm he is as a result of what he notices.

Perhaps this could be taken as empirical support for the claim that attention is more important than retribution or attempts at deterrence or reform.

Attending to people in this way is closely related to taking them seriously. We take children seriously when, amongst other things, we take note of their interests and problems and allow them a say in what happens to them. In this respect punishment takes the individual more seriously than manipulative modes of treatment, certainly, but as we have seen the punishments of institutions like schools risk being seen as merely part of an irrelevant, self-contained game if the rules they enforce become too remote from the values and interests of those required to obey them. I take a child seriously when instead of automatically punishing him for repeatedly failing to do his maths homework I take the trouble (perhaps instead, perhaps in addition) to find out why he doesn't do his maths. In a dozen other ways we can take children more seriously than we do in schools. We can give them a say in designing the rules by which the school or class is run; we can, in questioning and in discussions, look for meaning and relevance in the points they make and the answers they give rather than looking for what we have already decided is the relevant point or the 'right' answer.

To take children seriously is not necessarily, as some adults fear, to concede them too much power by regarding their desires and interests as authoritative. Taking a person seriously is a matter of understanding and acknowledging his interests: it does not mean gratifying them. Paradoxically, we do that when we manipulate, when we devote our energy to anticipating children's more superficial and transient urgings. In this respect manipulation can correctly be described as slavish. To take children seriously is no more than to accept them as people in their own right instead of as projections of our own needs and fears. We treat children as persons in this regard when, for example, we allow that their accounts of their own experience of the world – in being frightened by the dark, for example, or in finding school boring – are not to be dismissed in favour of our adult, official versions of how things really are: 'No you don't, dear', 'I'm sure school's fun really'. Leila Berg (1977) describes in chilling detail how some adults feel compelled to force their own vision of how the world *ought* to be on children while insisting that this is in fact how it actually *is* for the child: this is the book you want, this is what you really mean, this is how you must be feeling. 'Everyone has experience – but teachers assess it, say whether it is worthwhile experience (when they agree it happened) or unapproved experience (which is then called no experience and has not happened)' (ibid., p. 121).

I have been critical (and shall be again) of the Kantian tradition in ethics. But Kant himself had some valuable things to say about our relationships with other people. In a famous passage he wrote that the attitude we owe them is like the respect or reverence we ought to feel for the moral law: respect for a worth that thwarts or chastens our self-love (*Groundwork*, para. 16n.). Like morality, other people are something I have not invented and do not own. They are separate, something quite apart that I must take account of, in no way a function of my own wishes. I am to view others not as means to any ends of my own but as ends in themselves: I can value them precisely because they are *others*, different from myself.

This has perhaps been one of the less influential parts of Kant's ethical theory. Michael Marland dedicates *The Craft of the Classroom* to 'the pupils I have taught, still teach, and will teach, whom I have learnt to like more as I have learnt to manage them better'. I am reminded of Blake's Little Black Boy, who looks forward to equality with the English child in heaven:

> And then I'll stand and stroke his silver hair,
> And be like him and he will then love me.
> (The Little Black Boy, in *Songs of Innocence*)

When we thus do not regard others as fully persons our sense of ourselves as persons is impaired in the end, for much of our status as persons depends on the relationships we enter into with other people. If many teachers find little enduring satisfaction in their work perhaps it is partly because by diminishing their pupils to the status of an inferior class of beings, likeable only when they are 'managed', they diminish themselves.

9

Responsibility

A recurring theme of this book has been the value of treating people, including children, as free and responsible beings. It was this, for example, that manipulation was said to violate and that any philosophy of punishment must accommodate. In these last two chapters I try to provide an account first of responsibility and then of freedom.

Here I want to tackle three questions in particular about responsibility. What is it, in general, to be responsible? Can we treat children as fully responsible persons, or is to be a child to occupy an inferior status in this respect? What is involved in regarding responsibility as a virtue?

There are three rather different, though related, senses of 'responsibility' in these questions. The first is the sense in which to ask if someone is responsible is to ask whether he has the capacities of a normal human being, whether he is a person in the full sense and whether he is worthy of being treated as our equal in essential respects. The second sense is that in which it is possible to ask, of someone who is thought to be a responsible person in the first sense, whether on some particular occasion he was really responsible for his actions. There are circumstances in which a mature, rational and capable person might not be held to be responsible for what he did: if his car went out of control and caused an accident purely because of a mechanic's incompetence, for instance, or if he was tortured or put under intolerable psychological pressure. The third sense is that in which we might say we admired somebody for acting so responsibly, or in which we might believe that people ought to learn to take responsibility for their own lives. (The first two senses correspond roughly to what Hart, 1968, calls respectively capacity-responsibility and liability-responsibility.)

To treat someone as responsible in the first sense is to regard him as one who has acted knowingly and willingly, who could have acted otherwise. A responsible person has the capacity to make choices, to deliberate and act deliberately. The actions he performs are done under one intention or another, even if the intention is not always explicit: they are responses to the world as viewed under some description, rather than mere reflexes. Thus when I laugh more is involved than the rictus of my lips and the contractions of my diaphragm: I laugh because I see what you said as amusing, or I laugh in order to put you at your ease (or, perhaps, to irritate or wound you). The actions of a responsible agent fit into a story in which items of behaviour have meaning which is conferred upon them by the intentions of agents and the interpretations of those intentions by spectators and those to whom the actions are done.

Somebody who was not a responsible person in this sense, through being severely brain-damaged, perhaps, would not be a candidate for punishment or blame at all. Perhaps thorough-going determinism of the sort that would absolve us altogether from responsibility of this kind is attractive to some people precisely because it seems to promise a world without punishment, blame or guilt. But it would be a world without praise as well, for if people are not responsible what they do aright will be just as much something they are caused to do, and so cannot be praised for, as what they do amiss. In fact it is hard to see how even the idea of doing something well or aright could then have any meaning. There could be no such thing as courage, either, in a world without responsibility, for to display courage rather than recklessness is to appreciate the danger yet choose to act despite it for the sake of some greater good. (If this means that many of the actions which are commonly regarded as heroic and awarded medals are not really acts of courage at all then I think it is the medals rather than the analysis of courage which have to go.) Nor could there be qualities such as mercy or justice, for these and other virtues imply some degree of choice or decision, and it is the real possibility of this choice or decision that determinism denies. A world without responsibility in this sense, then, is one which does not appear very attractive when we look at it closely. More than this, it is scarcely conceivable. A world in which we did not through our intentions confer meaning on our own actions and by inference read meaning into other people's would be sufficiently unlike any world we could understand to justify us calling such a state of affairs logically impossible. That is, it is no more possible that creatures like us could live in such a world than we could a world where things had the property of being in several places at once.

We value being treated as responsible persons because it is emasculating and humiliating when others do not respect our capacity to originate and confer our own meanings: witness the rage we may feel when somebody disregards our viewpoint or dismisses it as merely caused or determined, the kind of view we would of course hold being a woman, or middle-class, or a child. In addition responsibility is connected with other virtues such as equality and fairness: it is unjust to impose our own views on a responsible person who has his own viewpoint on the world. This is to treat him as less than an equal, to fail to accord him the same respect we extend to those we do not similarly impose upon (cf. Dworkin, 1977, ch. 6).

Where do children stand in all this? On the one hand many of our attitudes and practices suggest we think of children as fully responsible persons, in the capacity sense. We do not hesitate to praise or blame even very small children, calling them good or kind or naughty, and the feelings we may entertain towards their displays of these qualities – we may be angry, shocked, indignant, proud, pleased, relieved and so on – argue that we are indeed viewing the child as a moral being and not as one whom we simply hope to condition for the future by the association of certain words with smacks or rewards. Even before he can speak a child can perceive meaning in another's actions, seeing a gesture, for example, as comforting or threatening. Similarly he can confer meaning, intending to hurt or to bestow affection. He has a distinct viewpoint on the world that can be insulted, for instance if he senses that his routine is being disturbed purely to suit the convenience of his parents.

On the other hand, it might be argued, children lack the extent of knowledge that would enable them to make realistic choices and decisions. It might also be maintained that they are subject to deficiencies of the will as well as those of knowledge or rationality, for instance that they find it harder to adhere to their decisions and perhaps cannot resist the promptings of immediate wants and urges as well as an adult usually can. They also lack all sorts of important skills and 'know-how': how to cope with those who would abuse or exploit them, how to find their way around the forms, regulations and administrative machinery that increasingly dominate our lives. We seem to acknowledge these shortcomings in setting ages below which a child is not legally responsible for his actions, may not be a party to a legal contract, and so on. This second account gives a truer picture of the position of children in our society. As John Harris (1982) puts it, there is an 'almost universally held belief that children are incompetent to exercise the responsibilities and discharge the obligations of citizenship', that is those of persons in the full sense.

Of course it is perfectly possible to dispute this picture. Harris

95

(ibid.) argues that children are capable of planning systematic policies and strategies requiring a high degree of rationality; he thinks it is far from clear 'that those who do not have such an ability would not rapidly develop it if permitted, or forced by the experience from which adults protect them, so to do'. He observes that 'Many children are first-rate mechanics and electricians, not to mention musicians, athletes and so on'. We might add that though it is easy to think of kinds of know-how that children tend to lack it is equally easy to think of ones where they are likely to be superior to the average adult: computer skills, for example, which could hardly be dismissed as a trivial area of competence. Moreover in the area of social skills quite a small child, so far from being inept and vulnerable, may be more successful than its parents – in getting its own way, for example, or in making friends.

It looks as if the question of how far children can be considered responsible persons is susceptible to endless debate, especially since the evidence that can be adduced by both sides is so diverse. Is there any relatively uncontentious criterion or set of criteria here? I want to discuss one answer that has commonly been given recently. It derives from the work of psychologists, notably Jean Piaget and Lawrence Kohlberg. Reference to psychology should not seem out of place in a book whose orientation is philosophical. Philosophers of the school that concentrates on 'linguistic analysis' might disagree, but there are other styles of philosophy. In any case certain ideas from psychology have already penetrated quite deeply into educational philosophy, as I shall indicate, and cannot be ignored.

Piaget and Kohlberg have attempted to distinguish a number of stages or phases in children's moral and intellectual development whose order is invariable since each stage can occur only by building on the one before it. Thus Piaget calls the period from birth to 18 months, approximately, the sensori-motor stage, that from 18 months to roughly 6 or 7 years the pre-operational stage, that from then until about 11 years the concrete operational stage and the last stage, which begins at about 11 years, that of formal operations. What these stages are supposed to involve is conveniently summarized by Margaret Donaldson (1978, pp. 129 ff.). During the pre-operational stage, for example, the child is held to be unable to cope with tasks like conservation, as when water is poured from a squat, fat container into a tall, thin one and the child cannot grasp that the amount of water is the same; or tasks of class inclusion, when the child cannot perceive the relation between a whole and its parts, for instance. Thus when the child is asked, of a picture showing one white and two red flowers, whether there are more red flowers than flowers he replies that there are.

Piagetian developmental psychology appears to provide us with a schema for classifying children's level of competence. Even if the ages referred to are only approximations it looks as if we can say with some confidence that there are fundamental and important things which a child of 14 years can be expected to be able to do but not one of, say, 8 years. The older child can reason logically, entertain hypotheses, deduce consequences and treat ideas as ideas rather than as standing directly for observable things. So he or she can solve problems of the type: Peter is taller than John but smaller than Mark – who is the tallest of the three? with reference to the logic of the question rather than by thinking of the Peters and Johns that he or she actually knows. The implications of Piaget's work are particularly damaging to our general view of the competence of young children. His claims suggest that 'the child under the age of 7 is in many ways extremely limited in his ability to think and reason' (Margaret Donaldson, 1978, pp. 33–4); that 'children under the age of 6 or 7 are very bad at communicating' (ibid., p. 18) because they are 'egocentric' or unable to see the world from another person's point of view. The very titles of the stages, such as 'pre-operational', suggest that the child's intellectual status is best understood and even defined by its being essentially only a preparation for, and so is necessarily inferior to, that of the adult.

Kohlberg has built on Piaget's work in the area of moral development. The result can be conveniently summarized by quoting an educational philosopher much influenced by work in developmental psychology:

There is a general consensus that children pass through various stages in their conception of rules which is independent of the content of the rules concerned. They pass from regarding conformity to rules purely as a way of avoiding punishment and obtaining rewards to a level at which rules are regarded as entities in themselves that are just 'there' and which emanate from the collective will of the group and from people in authority. They finally pass to the level of autonomy, when they appreciate that rules are alterable, that they can be criticised and should be accepted or rejected on a basis of reciprocity and fairness. (Peters, 1973, p. 130)

This means, of course, that the moral thinking of the child should not properly be called *moral* thinking at all: rather the child thinks first in purely prudential and conventional terms and moral understanding is only very gradually differentiated from this. It seems fair to sum up Kohlberg's and Piaget's work in this field as

97

implying that 'young children lack moral understanding . . . children's judgements are dominated by nonmoral appraisals and true moral understanding only comes about after a gradual process of separating nonmoral judgements from moral ones' (Shweder *et al.*, 1981, p. 288).

If this was correct there would be far-reaching implications for our view of the child and we would indeed have a powerful criterion for distinguishing responsible persons from others. For we would have to regard the child's capacity for responsibility – for deliberating on moral matters, making choices in the moral area and so on – as essentially undeveloped, a mere shadow of what can only be fully realized in an adult or sophisticated adolescent (though Kohlberg is not confident that many adults ever do reach the final stage of fully autonomous morality). We could not think of a child as entirely the bearer of his *own* intentions or the conferrer of his *own* meanings on the world while he was still at a level where he saw right and wrong as undifferentiated from what brings him praise and punishment or from what existing rules and conventions enjoin: what Kohlberg calls 'goodboy' and 'authority-oriented' levels of morality. Moreover, if one level of moral understanding has to be consolidated properly before the next and more mature level can develop out of it we might conclude that the best thing for well-intentioned adults to do is to provide an environment appropriate to each stage: plenty of rewards and punishments to provide the backing for rules, followed by emphasis on conformity for the sake of peer-group solidarity or plain respect for authority 'as such'. This is precisely the conclusion that Peters draws:

> [the] attempt to arrange an institution so that its control system is not out of tune with stages of development seems eminently sensible. . . . The Public Schools, who specialised in character-training, implicitly acknowledged this; for they combined an appeal to team spirit and to authority-based rule-conformity for all, with an emphasis on independence of mind and sticking to principles for those more senior boys who were singled out to command rather than simply to obey. (1973, pp. 132, 135)

And Peters thinks that 'progressive educators' have been insufficiently aware of the facts of moral development, requiring children so to speak to run autonomously before they have learned to walk with the help and under the direction of adults.

It would be easy to demonstrate how many educational philosophers have seized on the work of Piaget and Kohlberg as providing empirical support for philosophical theses about morality and moral learning (for a good recent example, see Straughan, 1982a, esp. pp. 7 ff.). The attraction of Kohlberg's account in particular is no doubt its similarity in certain respects to that given by Kant, who writes (especially in the *Groundwork*) as if only actions done autonomously can have specifically moral worth, those coloured by what he calls 'empirical motives' such as desires or feelings having no truly moral value at all. The neo-Kantianism of much recent philosophy of education could only appear to be confirmed by a psychology which saw the adult's autonomy and rationality as developing out of the heteronomous appraisals and egocentric fumblings of childhood.

It is therefore of the greatest importance that recent work in psychology has begun to cast serious doubt on the picture of the child's competence drawn by Piaget and Kohlberg. For example, certain of Piaget's experiments appeared to show that a 'pre-operational' child could not work out what perspective a doll had of three model mountains it was placed among: the child, it seemed, imagined the doll saw the mountains in the way they appeared from where the child himself was sitting. This was taken as evidence of the 'egocentricity' or inability to 'decentre' of the pre-operational child. However, when the context is that of a game in which the doll is hiding from a policeman, a context which involves feelings and intentions the child can understand and so *makes sense* to him, the child's ability to grasp different perspectives is greatly increased (Hughes and Donaldson, 1979). Similarly there is now evidence that even 4 year olds can cope with inclusion problems (such as the question whether there are more red flowers than flowers) when the problem is presented so as to make clear exactly what comparison the experimenter is asking the child to make (McGarrigle *et al.*, 1978). In summarizing a lot of recent work of this tendency Margaret Donaldson (1978) writes:

> Children are not at any stage as egocentric as Piaget has claimed . . . the gap between children and adults is not so great in this respect as has recently been widely believed. . . . Children are not so limited in ability to reason deductively as Piaget – and others – have claimed . . . at least from age 4 then, we must again acknowledge that the supposed gap between children and adults is less than many people have claimed. (pp. 58–9)

Similarly in the moral area it is now being plausibly maintained that even 4 to 6 year olds possess 'an intuitive moral competence that displays itself in the way they answer questions about moral rules and in the way they excuse their transgressions and react to the transgressions of others' (Shweder *et al.*, 1981). According to this view, Piaget and Kohlberg confused stages in the ability to articulate and reflect upon the formal principles of morality with stages in the development of the moral understanding itself. So far from children's judgements being dominated by non-moral forms of appraisal, they in fact distinguish between social or conventional rules, which they regard as changeable, relative to context and based on consensus, and moral ones, which they do not perceive as deriving their force from social context or agreement. 'Moral rules were evaluated on the basis of factors intrinsic to acts, such as harm inflicted on others and violation of rights' (Weston and Turiel, 1980).

We cannot then simply accept as proven and uncontroversial the picture of children as inadequate in some basic and far-reaching sense, either in the domain of rationality in general or that of morality in particular. What the studies I have cited above suggest is that children may be less sophisticated in the way they discuss, rationalize and reflect on their moral intuitions and experiences, as well as less able to exercise certain intellectual abilities in contexts where the usual human background of feeling and emotion is absent: notably the 'artificial' environment set up by a psychologist conducting an experiment. We might go so far as to conclude that it reflects rather well, instead of badly, on children that they function best where the normal background conditions of human life are present, and that they find such a question as 'Are there more red flowers than flowers?' puzzling and answer it, charitably, as if it were a different question that made more sense. There is no justification that I can see for consigning children to an inferior status on the basis of their unfamiliarity with certain sorts of highly unusual contexts or even their relative inability to articulate their moral intuitions. Such failings are nowhere near as basic as those Piaget and Kohlberg seemed to be identifying and in any case they will be found among many older persons whom we would not hesitate to classify as full adult.

If we must revise our understanding of developmental psychology in this way then the case for paternalism in the treatment of children – the view that we are justified in intervening in their lives, even against their will, for their own good – is correspondingly weakened. The question of paternalism is not removed altogether, however, for even if we consider children fully responsible in the capacity sense there are still likely to be many particular occasions on which it seems obvious to us that a child lacks sufficient experience or understanding and we have to decide just how far this warrants us as adults in acting for his own good rather than allowing him to make his own mistakes. Cases here will range from those which strike us as very clear-cut, such as the 5 year old who runs out into the busy road or his older brother who decides to experiment with glue-sniffing, to ones where it is not nearly so obvious what is and what is not in the child's interest. Do we override the 10 year old's considered judgement that he would rather give up piano lessons, or a 15 year old's decision to abandon serious interest in school work and pin all her hopes on a career as a model or rock singer? Are there, that is, any general limits we can draw to the extent to which we are willing to give children responsibility for their own lives?

We might try first to justify intervention in those cases where there is reason to believe the individual concerned will later agree we were right to do so: the reluctant pianist will thank us when he's an accomplished performer, just as the thwarted glue-sniffer will be grateful when he understands that he might have caused himself irreparable brain-damage. The trouble with this criterion is that it simply assumes that the judgement of the older person (here, the same person when he is older) is automatically more reliable. This may not be so, not least because our interventions may work like self-fulfilling prophecies and create the consent they anticipate. This might happen if we engender a taste or interest by our interventions, such as a passion for computer-programming: once the pupil is happily addicted we cannot adduce this as evidence that we were right all along. He might have been happier still, or those around him might have been happier and his life been better balanced, if we had introduced him to something else. Perhaps too there are times in education when a young person is forced to invest so much in his education that it becomes difficult for him to do other than insist the investment was worthwhile: he has identified himself with the process to such an extent that he cannot stand back from it and see its faults. Here too we would be right to distrust subsequent consent.

Instead of trying to justify intervention on the grounds of subsequent consent we might turn to hypothetical consent: the idea that consent would be given if the person concerned were, say, fully informed and fully rational. This might justify us in those cases where we interfere by informing someone that he has chosen the wrong means to his intended end or that his action will have consequences he has not foreseen. But these cases are not the problem. The difficulty is less how we are to justify giving someone information to help him achieve his existing goals than how we are to justify imposing on him different goals altogether. What counts as rational or as rationality is itself highly contentious. There is

101

probably no infringement of others' rights so gross that it cannot be defended in the name of some version of rationality or another. I return to the relationship between freedom and rationality in the next chapter.

One last justification of paternalism in education worth considering briefly here is the idea that we may intervene with requirements that serve to expand educational opportunities but not ones that would restrict them. We are justified, that is, in overriding children's choices where in the long term this has the effect of expanding their capacity for choice. Arguments along these lines can be found in J. P. White (1973) and Gutman (1980). White draws a distinction between activities such as maths or art where you need to have engaged in the activity to understand properly what it is and so what you are rejecting, if you do reject it, and other activities, like cookery or accountancy, where no such depth of acquaintance is necessary before making a choice. The implication is that if children are to grow up free to make their own decisions on what place mathematics or art are to have in their lives they must first, under compulsion if necessary, have got to know what they involve. One problem with this kind of argument is that it either takes for granted that activities such as maths and art are sufficiently important, something like areas of understanding that constitute the developed mind of a fully rational chooser, or requires a theory such as Hirst's 'forms of knowledge' thesis (see above, p. 49) to support it. This returns us to the difficult question of the nature of rationality. In any case, as Harris (1982) observes, any argument which rests the case for paternalism on the grounds of expansion of future opportunities for children 'makes impossible the rational relinquishing of such control at any time prior to death'. The argument is too powerful: it would justify compulsory schooling for all, adults included, until they could demonstrate that they understood what mathematics, or the physical sciences or philosophy, involve.

To hold that it is very difficult to make out a sound general case for paternalism towards children is not to abandon them to whatever may happen. It is not to believe that an adult ought to stand by while they drink bleach or run out into the road or do themselves other sorts of substantial or irreparable harm. It is only to maintain that there ought to be a presumption in favour of allowing children, like adults, to take responsibility for their own lives. The onus is then on those who want to take that responsibility away, and employ compulsion and coercion, to make out a good case for doing so. I suspect that case is often harder to make out than we think, particularly in education, where compulsion often serves merely to persuade children that behind the requirement that they learn such-and-such or obey some rule or other there lies no really good reason but only the mysterious, arbitrary will of the teacher.

In spite of all that I have written so far of the merits of treating people as responsible beings, responsibility, I am aware, sounds a sombre and unattractive kind of ideal. We tend to regard responsibility in general as a burden. That is surely because it has become too closely tied in our thinking to meeting the expectations of others and particularly to playing roles in which our part is to be answerable to someone else, usually someone above us in a hierarchy. (Hart, 1968, p. 213, appears to think responsibility as a virtue invariably involves reference to role-responsibility.) Thus as a teacher you are responsible to the headmaster, he in turn is responsible to the school governors and the local authority, and so on. Too often being responsible in this sense turns out simply to be a matter of doing as you are told: 'try to be more responsible' may be just a more pompous and moralistic way of saying 'don't do that'. When teacher tells the children 'I expect you to behave responsibly while I'm out of the room' they are not pleased that he is treating them as adults. They know that this amounts to an order to keep to ill-defined rules which they will be both punished and made to feel guilty (as lacking in adult capacities) for breaking.

Of course those responsibilities which are connected to roles are not unimportant. A large part in our estimation of a person is played by how seriously he takes his responsibilities as father or employee or committee member. But, *pace* Hart (above), this cannot exhaust the notion of responsibility as a virtue. For we do not think of the concentration camp guard who did his appointed job diligently and was a loving father to his children as a model of responsibility. The reason for this is that we have the further responsibility to decide just what roles we will fill in life, what we will make of those particular duties and responsibilities we find the world expects us to shoulder:

Helmer: This is disgraceful. Is this the way you neglect your most sacred duties?

Nora: What do you consider is my most sacred duty?

Helmer: Do I have to tell you that? Isn't it your duty to your husband and children?

Nora: I have another duty, just as sacred.

Helmer: You can't have. What duty do you mean?

Nora: My duty to myself.

(Ibsen, *A Doll's House*, Act III)

Nora's 'duty to herself' here is not a selfish sort of concern, nor is it a duty to be weighed *alongside* that to her family. It is what we might call

103

the higher-order duty or responsibility to examine the shape and balance of her life, including all its separate role-responsibilities, as a whole. She tells Helmer: 'I can't be satisfied any longer with what most people say, and what's in books. I must think things out for myself and try to understand them.' It is for failing to do this (amongst other things) that we condemn the concentration camp guard: he took refuge in the role he was allotted and did not exercise his capacity for independent choice and evaluation, for considering whether it was right to accept that particular sort of role-responsibility, even if this meant disobeying orders.

To be responsible in this sense, then, is to examine your commitments and engagements to see if they are such as you really want to endorse as your own. It is to take responsibility for your own life: to be truly the author of your actions and the possessor of your own ideas rather than one who, as Ibsen's Nora had been, takes them uncritically from other people or from books. There is a connection here with the notion of giving an answer or account, which is sometimes said (for example by Haydon, 1978) to be the idea that holds together the different senses of 'responsibility'. For to take responsibility for your own life is to be able to account to others for what you do with answers that are truly your *own* in that you have thought them through for yourself and are willing to defend them in argument. There is also a connection with my earlier analysis of authority. People who take responsibility for their own lives will be inclined to justify themselves with reference to those standards of correctness appropriate to what they are doing, rather than by invoking 'higher authority' in the shape of persons or regulations that they have taken orders from. Being thus able to *give an account* is to be able to give reasons that 'hold their own' in argument or are rooted in those networks of reasons that we call disciplines, subjects or traditions. Galileo accounted for planetary motion in scientific terms and so did not feel answerable to the Inquisition; Socrates experienced the insistence of his own *daimon* or critical faculty as more powerful than the state's demand for religious conformity. It required a more rigorous answer in the form of an account of the moral life that would hold up under philosophical scrutiny.

As these two examples suggest, taking responsibility for your own life may be difficult and uncomfortable. Equally, however, it can be a releasing and liberating project, as a person comes slowly to feel less dependent on the approval of those others, real, imagined or 'internalized', the voices of parents or teachers, perhaps, whose supposed displeasure was a source of guilt. Such a person is less 'driven' and more in control of his own destiny. It is also liberating to learn that there are limits to your responsibility: that there were perfectly good reasons why you were never able to take advantage of certain opportunities, for example. An ethic of responsibility does not require us to carry the world on our shoulders.

In schools we lay the foundations for children to come to take responsibility for their own lives when we help them to take responsibility for their own learning. The first step (in order of importance, if not of time) in doing this is to make minimal use of extrinsic rewards and punishments, for a child who is motivated purely by these has the area in which he can make choices and take decisions severely limited. Where extrinsic motivation seems unavoidable it should be overt, for the child who knows he must either work or be punished has the responsibility for this decision at least left open to him. This is essentially to repeat my earlier points about manipulation. A person who is manipulated to the extent of his very wants and interests being the result of others bending him to their purposes has no important decisions or choices to make.

Part of encouraging a child to take responsibility for his own learning, then, is to release him from feeling that he is answerable to *you*. The other part is to help him to see that he is essentially answerable to himself: it is he, first and foremost, that stands to benefit from learning, in that education is *the* process by which human beings make sense of their world and acquire some understanding of what it is to lead a full and satisfying life. But this means of course that what goes on in schools will have to be of a genuinely educational nature, or the business of helping pupils to take responsibility for their own learning will be a fraud and a sham. You cannot hope that children will come to be motivated by the intrinsic interest of their work if you offer them nothing interesting to work on. You cannot expect them to see that education exists to connect with and enhance their lives if the conditions of their schooling are such as to suggest that they are rather contemptible creatures of low status, fit only to be herded from one drab, uninspiring classroom to another. You cannot imagine they will try to find significance in their learning when it appears to them that all the significant and important learning has been done by others (James Watt, Marco Polo, teacher and whoever wrote the textbook) while their role is just to accept the results.

Conceptions of education and responsibility, that is, go hand-in-hand. One educational philosopher offers it as a definition that 'Teaching occurs when one person consciously accepts responsibility for the learning of another' (Langford, 1968, p. 114). I would not disagree. But might we not think of *educative* teaching as the business of helping other people take responsibility for their *own* learning?

10

Freedom and Education

Like responsibility, freedom is something we seem to value without always having a very clear idea of what it is. The purpose of this final chapter is to distinguish some different kinds of freedom and to make out a case for one particular kind, the freedom to discover and act on your important or significant purposes, as being required by the educational values I have argued for in this book.

The first and most obvious point to make about freedom and liberty (I shall use these words as synonyms) is that they tend to be used as terms of propaganda. All sorts of groups and political parties claim them in order to lend legitimacy to their cause. Western democracies call themselves the 'free world', while their opponents retort that such liberties as our freedom of speech and freedom to vote are not worth much where ignorance and manipulation by commercial interests induce 'false consciousness' on the part of the masses. Some believe that *true* freedom is to be found in the sort of collective endeavour that 'communism' originally labelled. Virtually any demand for anything can be called a 'liberation' movement. For example, there was a fashion some years ago for certain sorts of shoplifters to say they were 'liberating' what they stole, on the grounds presumably that 'property is theft'. The absurdity of this was well caught by a contemporary cartoon which showed a young man outside a bookshop complaining to a friend: 'I just went in to liberate a few books and when I came out some bastard had pinched my bike.'

One response to the looseness with which the word 'freedom' is often used is to insist on the importance of specifying what you want freedom *from* and what you want freedom *to do*. Thus it makes for clarity if someone demanding the liberation of women, for instance, spells out that they want freedom to enter professions and institutions that they have been barred from, or freedom from sexual harassment in the workplace, freedom from economic exploitation in the shape of equal wages to men's, and so on. This insistence however has a way of sliding into a rather different claim: that these various freedoms *from* and *to* are really all that freedom amounts to, that there is no single kind of thing that you can be demanding in the name of freedom as there is when you ask for more jobs or a new by-pass.

Something like this claim is usually part of what is often called (most notably by Berlin, 1969) the negative view of freedom. The negative view (there are none of the normal pejorative connotations of 'taking a negative view' here) regards freedom essentially as the individual's independence of interference by others. Freedom of speech, of movement, freedom from arbitrary arrest, from cruel and unusual forms of punishment, and other liberties tending to be found in civilized countries are the product of this conception of liberty. The strength of the negative view is largely precisely this: that it is the philosophical and political source of some beneficial freedoms that we are inclined to take for granted but quickly notice when they are infringed or removed. Those who support the negative view see their task principally as defining the area in which the individual is to be left free from interference. When does my liberty to conduct my life in the way I wish become incompatible with others' liberty to do the same, and perhaps justify the state or other agencies in intervening? At the time I write this some people's freedom of movement around the country is held in many quarters to be incompatible with the freedom of others to earn a lawful living: 'flying pickets' are turned back by police in order to protect others' 'right to work'. And one reason why this causes controversy is that freedom of movement and association is one of the particular freedoms traditionally safeguarded by the negative view. (This is not to say, of course, that even on that view it is an inviolable freedom, especially when it conflicts with other traditional liberties.)

One consequence of the negative view is that freedom is not the highest good. It is merely an instrumental one: it makes possible the pursuit and enjoyment of such other goods as a person, rendered free from interference, chooses. Thus J. S. Mill, commonly regarded as one of the founding fathers of this view, often writes as if the value of liberty is that it tends to promote such qualities as individuality or diversity (*On Liberty*, ch. 3).

Opponents of the negative view tend to observe that many of these particular freedoms are rather hollow for many people. Freedom in choice of schools, for example, is only effective for those with the money to purchase private education or to move house into different areas, or at least with the confidence to examine various schools, interview headteachers and so on. Freedom of speech and freedom to vote do not mean much if you are wholly unable to gain access to important sorts of knowledge or incapable of shaking off habits of deference to authority. These freedoms, as it is sometimes put, may be more formal than actual. The negative view may seem to propose a rather heartless outlook where people are abandoned to their endemic poverty or to the traditionally limited ambitions of their class or caste, all in the name of freedom. 'Responsibility' is suspect as a political slogan for the same reason.

This is the kind of thinking that may fuel the opposite or positive conception of freedom. The central idea here is that true freedom consists in putting the control of an individual's or a nation's destiny in the appropriate hands. This may be God ('whose service is perfect freedom'), the Party (Freedom is Slavery, ran the slogan on the Ministry of Truth in Orwell's *Nineteen Eighty-Four*), a particular element, such as rationality, in the individual's mental life, or any number of other versions. It takes some of its strength from the fact that though the negative view allows a person's own wants to be authoritative in the area of his life left free from interference, we are inclined to believe that the new sciences of sociology and psychology have taught us how many of his wants may not be so much truly his *own* as ones he has been caused to have or has taken over automatically together with his membership of a particular class or culture. On the other hand, the positive view seems to have the consequence that people can be forced to be free: they can be compelled to defer to the leadership of whoever or whatever it is whose authority constitutes 'true' freedom. That seems unacceptable, and from that follows much of the unpopularity of the positive view (the view is attacked in detail and with great vigour by Berlin, 1969). But perhaps we ought not to dismiss the positive view too rapidly. After all, the idea that people should take responsibility for their own lives and learning, which I argued for in the previous chapter, looks as if it belongs with positive views, as do all suggestions that there is value in autonomy or in people ruling themselves in one way or another. For these are answers to the question, in whose hands shall control over our lives be put? Yet these are obviously not cases of giving up control of your life to some *other* agency and calling the outcome 'freedom'. I shall defend my own version of a positive view presently.

First, however, it is important to see what implications these views hold for education. The negative view might appear to suggest that the fewer restrictions there are on you the more freedom you have, so that the ideal condition is one of total removal of restrictions. From here it is a short step to the notion that it is a cruel constraint on a child to bring it up in a particular culture or to speak

108

a particular language: that the ideal is to subject it to as few influences as possible and so give it maximum freedom to choose its own lines of development. What is wrong with this is convincingly put by Mary Midgley (1980). Quite simply, we *need* a culture, a world of particulars to grow up in. A person brought up so far as possible without a culture or with a smattering of many (some poor rich child, perhaps, trailing behind jet-setting parents in the care of a succession of nannies) would not be in an unusually good position to choose. The opposite, in fact: he or she would have no real grasp of what the alternatives amounted to. As far as learning to choose is concerned we cut our teeth on the culture we find around us, which is of course not to deny it may be an impoverished one or one we come to feel we would rather not have been born into. 'Culture is not opposed to freedom. It makes it possible' (ibid., p. 287).

This analysis suggests that there is something wrong in general with the idea that the fewer restrictions there are the more freedom you automatically have. What is missing is a sense of the *significance* of different freedoms. Ancient Sparta probably presented its citizens with far fewer restrictions than the modern UK (no licensing hours, double yellow lines, rules relating to fire precautions in public buildings . . .) yet we do not therefore think of Sparta as a model of the free society. That is because it did not allow some of the freedoms that we value most: the freedom to live according to your own conception of the good life, for instance, was denied equally to those born into the militaristic ruling élite and to the helots doomed to hereditary slavery. We cannot, then, simply identify the ideal situation from the point of view of freedom with one where there are least restrictions. The restrictions we want to be rid of are those on our important or significant freedoms, whatever those are. From this it may follow that we have to forgo other freedoms in order to secure the ones that matter to us, as we are inclined for example to accept restrictions on how and where we may drive cars so that everyone may have the freedom to make journeys on the roads in greater safety. This is sometimes referred to as the 'paradox of freedom': restrictions are often required to create liberties.

There are two other reasons, particularly important as far as education is concerned, for regarding the negative view of freedom with caution. The first is that it gives us a curious picture of what is involved in choosing. I am free, in this view, when I am not subject to restrictions, and in this state I exercise my freedom in choosing how to act, what goods to select from those available in my world, very much in the manner of one entering a shop. But on what kind of grounds, by what sort of standards, do I make my choice? Once we introduce the idea of standards in this way we bring in the possibility that making decisions may often involve effort, an attempt to perceive those standards justly and clearly despite, for example, our propensity to deceive ourselves, to always take the easier course, and so on. We allow also the possibility that these standards or criteria may impress themselves on us so forcibly that we feel we effectively have no choice. Perhaps I am trying to decide whether to accept the job I have been offered: as I consider the matter more and more deeply, and examine how this job would fit with the kind of person I am and the direction my life is taking, it seems there is less and less a real choice to make. I may feel caught up by a sense of vocation, even though in all sorts of ways I do not really *want* the job (it's poorly paid, demanding and insecure). I suggest this picture of choosing is truer to our experience of the world than the negative view's picture in which choosing is like looking round a shop, a process in which we demonstrate our freedom by the more or less ungrounded movement of our will (a process seen at its most extreme in certain existentialist conceptions of freedom; see Mary Midgley, 1980, ch. 9, and Iris Murdoch, 1970, *passim* and esp. pp. 8–9). But if choosing is like this then we are moving towards a positive view of freedom. For we have had to make room for the role of something like our rational faculties in discerning the grounds or standards according to which choices are made, and this is close to saying we are free not just when we choose but when we do so under the control of reason.

The second reason for distrusting the negative view is close to the first. The only possible grounds for choosing on the negative view is the intensity of our wants: all we can do on entering the shop is to look at the goods and see how strongly we want this or that. Hence the loneliness of choice and the exercise of the will on this conception: no one can help me determine the relative strength of my wants any more than they can measure the intensity of my despair or sexual longing or the pain of my headache. But, as I have already observed, our wants are not authoritative in this way. To take examples from earlier chapters, children may seem to want, to be asking for, punishment when more careful consideration suggests they really want attention. People may crave authority when their fundamental desire is for a clear sense of direction in their lives. Sometimes, even, we come to feel that 'our' wants were not ours at all but the vicarious ambitions of parents or teachers or the fads and fashions of our contemporaries. This points to a very important reason for not equating freedom with being able to act according to your wants: it leaves no basis for objecting to manipulation, the deliberate creation or implanting of wants. If it was done early enough and thoroughly enough the victim would be acting as he wanted, but where another person or persons have caused him to have those wants for purposes of their own it seems quite wrong to say he is free.

We can begin to see here how theories of freedom are inseparable from theories of what it is to be a person. In general I think the negative view gives us a very thin and unsatisfactory picture of what it is to be a person. It does not do justice, for instance, to the richness and complexity of choice and deliberation. The emphasis is on the removal of external, public restraints, and issues in the private and personal domain, such as the problematic nature of wants, are correspondingly neglected. This is what we might expect in an age where overt actions on the public stage are all-important (behaviourist theories in philosophy and psychology: there is no 'ghost in the machine' and all aspects of intelligence and ability come down to 'skills'), where utilitarianism tends to flourish both in the general sense in which the only values which are admitted are the ones which can be readily quantified and in the more specialized, philosophical sense in which morality is regarded exclusively as a business of what takes place in public life (and not as connected importantly to how we regard or think of other people).

Recent philosophical writing about education has reacted strongly against aspects of the negative view. In particular it has been severely critical of those child-centred or libertarian theories of education which regard the current wants of the child as authoritative. It has tended to recognize that choosing is a complex business which 'should not be confused with the way of opting for things which is encouraged by advertising agencies' (Peters, 1966, p. 197), drawing attention to the danger that a child who is given freedom from teachers and other adults may simply be at the mercy of peer-group pressures (e.g. ibid., p. 195) and thus still unfree, the implication being that rules and constraints may be necessary to create certain freedoms (the 'paradox of freedom' again). In this, philosophy of education reveals once more its debt to the moral philosophy of Kant, who repudiated wants as 'heteronomous' motives which cannot be the inspiration of action with specifically moral worth. And in line with the Kantian tradition there has been considerable emphasis on *autonomy* as one of the important goals of education.

Now the demand for autonomy may amount to a number of rather different things. First it can be a matter of stressing the importance of a person's beliefs and actions being his own. In the case of the autonomous person they are not 'supplied to him ready-made as are those of the heteronomous man: they are *his*, because the outcome of a still-continuing process of criticism and re-evaluation' (Benn, 1976, p. 124). Here autonomy is close to, if not identical with, the

111

ideal of taking responsibility for one's own life that I discussed in the previous chapter.

Secondly, autonomy may be taken to involve centrally a person acting on *rules* or *principles* that he has thought through for himself. A city or state that is autonomous lays down its own laws (*nomoi*) rather than having them imposed by another power. Those impressed by etymology sometimes seem to want to place emphasis less on the idea of ownership than on that of what is owned: 'Autonomy implies the ability and determination to regulate one's life by rules which one has accepted for oneself' (Peters, 1966, p. 197). That Peters sees *rules* as having significance, and is not just making the point that to be autonomous is to make your rules (along with your actions and beliefs) your own, is shown by his citation in the next sentence of Piaget as having demonstrated that 'such an attitude towards rules is generally impossible before the age of about seven'. Again we see here the marriage of the Kantian tradition with recent developmental psychology. Acting on rules or principles is held to be morally significant because one who so acts guarantees that he is not being swayed by the whims, fancies and other 'heteronomous motives' of the moment. What worries me is that when autonomy is equated with acting on principles, albeit your own, a crucial but generally unacknowledged shift has been made towards a particular version of the positive view of freedom. Acting on principle is a sophisticated, abstract and highly rational business. The ability to follow rules is in fact sometimes said to be the essence of a rational creature, for it involves seeing particular instances as falling under more general or higher-order categories and concepts. Thus autonomy is linked to certain uses of rationality. This can be characterized as a positive view, since it means that the freedom which autonomy represents is taken to lie in putting control in certain hands – here those of the rational part of the personality or mind. Combined with Piagetian and Kohlbergian developmental psychology this seems to have the consequence indicated by Peters (above), that since, allegedly, children below a certain age are incapable of the appropriate conception of rules and principles they are incapable of acting autonomously.

From here it is a short step to a third version of autonomy. Here autonomy is held to lie in the exercise not just of reason, but reason in a highly specific form. In particular there is the thesis that a properly developed rationality consists in the articulation of a number of basic modes of understanding, areas of experience or forms of knowledge, so that a person cannot be truly autonomous if he has not acquired these. R. F. Dearden, in a volume significantly entitled *Education and Reason* (1972), writes that there is a good argument for choosing a certain group of curricular objectives, if autonomy is valued. Such an argument would advocate developing, to whatever degree might be possible in given circumstances, various basic forms of understanding, distinguished from each other along the lines indicated by Professor P. H. Hirst.

It is worth noting that the article in which Paul Hirst originally set out his 'forms of knowledge' thesis was entitled 'Liberal education and the nature of knowledge' (1965). There he wrote that the Greeks saw a *liberal* education as 'freeing the mind to function according to its true nature' and he endorsed a similar basis for liberal education in 'man's conception of the diverse forms of knowledge he has achieved'.

This thesis is questionable. It identifies a person with his mind, and his mind with its most abstract and intellectual operations. It is possible to argue that the thinking of an educated human being is best characterized in terms of other kinds of powers – its critical quality, for example, or capacity for receptivity, or its creativity – which cannot be obviously reduced to dimensions of rationality (cf. R. K. Elliott, 1975). What is the 'true nature' of mind, and what is it for the mind to function in accordance with this and so be free? Can we disentangle the complex intellectual, spiritual, moral and emotional capacities and needs of human beings neatly into those of the rational mind on the one hand and something like the realm of the spirit and the feelings on the other? If we argue, then, from the nature of a person or his mind we are not forced necessarily to adopt the excessively rationalistic picture of freedom drawn by Hirst, Dearden and others.

We have here the clearest illustration of how theories of freedom, of education and of what it is to be a person all hold implications for each other. It is important to notice that theories of freedom do not only, as we might expect, bear on questions of *how* in education – on issues like punishment and control – but also on questions of the curriculum, of *what* shall be taught. This is perhaps surprising, but as we have just seen it is indeed so. We may well feel something strange has happened in the course of moving from a premise about the value of freedom or autonomy to a conclusion that requires us to accept, still in the name of freedom, what amounts to detailed recommendations for the common core of the school curriculum. If freedom consists in developing a fully rational mind in the sense of being initiated into the 'forms of knowledge' then it appears to follow that children can be made free by compulsory initiation. The idea that people can be compelled to be free has an implausible ring to it.

Although I do not accept that freedom has to consist in being rational in anything like the way outlined above, still, as I have already argued, freedom is crucially connected to the giving of reasons. Reasons do not have to be 'explicit' (Chapter 5): they do not have to begin with 'because' and they do not have to be so authoritative as to terminate discussion. To give reasons is not to achieve freedom in virtue of entering the realm of rationality, as though by partaking of rationality in any of its forms (or 'forms') a person showed he was realizing his goal as a human being and was thereby free, having kicked loose of all contingent and unworthy influences. Why, then, are reasons so vital to freedom?

Consider again the Case of the Extraneous Comment from Chapter 1. Deliberating on how to react to this kind of incident, searching for reasons to justify one course of action rather than another, is a matter of stepping out of the role of one whose behaviour is merely a response to the superficial features of a situation and who may easily be manipulated by others controlling those features. Suppose, for example, that I tend to react more or less automatically to such interruptions to my lessons with a display of irritation: it may well be that certain pupils, not altogether consciously perhaps, begin to engineer such displays to break the monotony of the lesson or win the admiration of their friends. Thinking about the reasons for what I do requires me to step back from what is going on and examine it. The fact that such-and-such a situation tended to trigger a response on my part is now something that I take into account in my deliberations, and I am to this extent free of being 'triggered' or manipulated. Searching for reasons, then, involves my stepping back from the situations I find myself in and thus back from myself:

> The 'stepping back' from a response not yet given, the awareness of what one is doing to determine what one is going to do thereafter is characteristic of all our search for reasons. (Beck, 1975, p. 134)

I do not mean to imply that this 'stepping back' is easy, still less to assert as dogma that it is always available to us to the same extent in all circumstances. We do not simply decide to 'step back' and then leap clean into a state of freedom. Rather we can, slowly and perhaps with great difficulty, become more reflective persons, more inclined to scrutinize our engagements and motives and examine the reasons for our actions.

> To be reasonable is not something one decides to do tomorrow; it is a *way* of acting to be maintained, not an episode in a role to be assumed. It is a state of personal being expressed in how a man thinks, what ideals he pursues, and how he treats others. It

is not a single step that takes him from being an interesting mechanism to being a person, but an enlargement of the person by repeatedly stepping back from what is given, finished, and done. (ibid., pp. 137–8)

But why, it may still be asked, should I *want* to go in for this business of 'stepping back', especially since it turns out to be a lengthy and perhaps difficult, even painful, process? The answer is that this is what is involved in sorting out what I really want, what my significant ends and purposes are in life. Here it matters a great deal what kind of philosophical account of wants and feelings we accept. It seems to me that a person does not establish what he really wants simply by weighing up his desires and finding which is quantitatively the most powerful. This is part of the picture which represents choice and decision as like being in a shop. But feelings, wants and desires are not just what Taylor (1979) calls 'brute' phenomena, characterized only by their degree of intensity, as itches and headaches are. If they were, there would indeed be no way of assessing them and discriminating between them beyond making some essentially private comparison of twinges, thrills and stabs as we would if we were trying to decide whether our headache was worse than the pain in our stomach. Far from being 'brute', however, our feelings involve appraisals and perceptions. I experience fear, for example, because I see a situation, or a person or animal, as dangerous or alarming. I feel embarrassed, perhaps, where I believe I have said or done something inappropriate. These appraisals may be right or wrong: the animal may be harmless, my behaviour not the social *faux pas* I thought it was.

This is what is meant, then, by saying our feelings, wants and so on are not 'brute' as sensations are. Because our feelings are susceptible to correction in the light of our (or others') further appraisals we can see our feelings as more or less significant. And this is not a matter of just correctly observing their strength. My most powerful desire may be to stop revising for an exam and join my friends down the pub. The fact that I do not do this is not due to the desire to pass the exam being *stronger* (if it was, I would not feel so distracted) but to my seeing success in the exam as important to my long-term purposes. There are some things I do because they 'are of great significance to me, meet important, long-lasting needs, represent a fulfilment of something central to me, will bring me closer to what I really am' (Taylor, 1979, p. 188). I identify myself with these projects and ambitions, while I regard others of my desires as embodying a false view of what is important, of what matters to me, and come to think of them as fetters or obstructions. To be free in this sense is not to be hindered in my significant purposes, either by the interference of other persons or the obstruction of internal, motivational elements. Taylor (ibid.) calls the process of discovering what are one's significant purposes 'strong evaluation'. It is a reflective business in which a person distances himself or 'steps back' from his wants: it reminds us that, as I wrote in Chapter 2, people have depth.

Being free in this sense is thus bound up with developing a sense of one's identity. This fits with what seems to me to be a fact of our experience of choice and deliberation: often when we have thought long and hard about the issues that lie behind a choice we are confronted with we find that there is then no choice, no decision to make. 'By the time the moment of choice has arrived the quality of attention has probably determined the nature of the act' (Iris Murdoch, 1970, p. 67). This explains why to be predictable is not necessarily to weaken our claim to be free. Our choices flow from the sort of person we are, from the central purposes and ends we have, and our freedom lies not in being able to make arbitrary choices but in our capacity for reflecting on and modifying those ends and purposes on which our identity rests. We are responsible not just for separate, disconnected actions but for the sort of *character* we have, the life we lead.

We can now see more clearly why manipulation is so insidious and destructive: it frequently not only appeals to and strengthens those desires which do not fit in with a person's sense of his identity (he does not like to think of himself as a competitive person, for example, but he has quite a vigorous competitive streak which can easily be played upon) but even attempts to seduce by offering a ready-made, spurious sense of identity: it is familiar that the advertisements for a whole range of products from cigarettes to cars imply that the consumer buys with them a whole way of life. So manipulation encourages the growth of what we might call the 'false self' system, complexes of desires and wants which a person would not endorse as his own if he was to stand back and consider them, as well of course as making it much more difficult to stand back and reflect at all.

On both the negative view of freedom and the kind of positive view that sees freedom as rationality there is little scope for any deep or personal kind of reflection of the sort that 'stepping back' involves. The negative view, as I have mentioned, makes room only for the assessment of wants and desires on a quantitative basis: considering the significance of one's long-term purposes and so on is, on this view, no more than introducing another set of wants into the balance. On the kind of positive view I have alluded to there is really nothing to reflect on: what is significant for us is given a priori in the nature of rationality, acting in accordance with which is, for all human beings universally, the achievement of freedom – the freedom of the mind to realize its true nature.

For the same sorts of reasons these views also make it difficult to see how one person can by careful attention and communication *help* another to reflect more fruitfully on his wants and purposes and so arrive at a better understanding of what is significant in his life – a process which we might reasonably regard as an important part of education. On the negative view I am the final authority on my wants, just as I am on my hunger and my headache. Any evaluating or assessing of my wants I must necessarily do alone. On the positive view there is no need for anyone to attend to me, to engage with me as an individual and help me discover what I want or think significant. What is truly significant is known in advance of any wishes I might express, and my wants can be consigned to the periphery of education, to the clutter of 'options'. (Or, of course, they can be harnessed by some wiser person in order to lead or manipulate me in the right direction. Once we despise wants and feelings enough manipulation does not seem so disreputable.) So education becomes a matter either of standing aside helplessly and letting the other go his way, as in the wilder extremes of libertarianism, or of requiring his conformity to pre-ordained systems in the name of rationality.

If we look again at the business of giving reasons, however, we find good grounds for reaffirming the sense of education as a communal enterprise involving genuine dialogue between individuals. What is a good reason for me ought to be a good reason for you: whether it really is a good reason depends on how well it 'holds its own' in the dialogue between us. In the classic example from the first book of Plato's *Republic* that I have already cited Thrasymachus asserts that what is right is simply what accords with the will of the strongest. But in the discussion that follows his reasons do not hold their own and so are shown not to be good reasons. Or consider an example of Beck's (1975, p. 135). A teacher asks a child to complete the sequence 2, 4, 6, expecting the answer '8'. But the child replies '12', because '12 is to 6 as 4 is to 2'. As Beck points out, this is *a* right answer, but based on different reasons from the ones that the teacher would have given for *his* answer. Here the teacher learns that

his own good reason was not a good enough reason, and he can show the child that the child's good reason was not good enough, by showing him the difference between a progression and a proportion. Each learns something about himself, about the other, and about arithmetic. (ibid.)

Some reasons, of course, seem to hold their own in all discussions, or we cannot even conceive of them failing to do so. These are the hypotheses of science, the laws of mathematics and so on, and we come to think of them as impersonally valid. But we do not know what will happen in dialogues still to take place. A number of good scientific reasons ceased to hold their own, for example, when Einstein entered the discussion. That is why we do well to think of the principles of science as hypotheses.

Let me summarize the rather complex argument of the last few pages. Freedom is connected to 'stepping back' and giving reasons, in the sense described, and also to discovering your significant and enduring purposes, a conception of your identity. You can benefit from association with other people in achieving such freedom first because of the dialectical nature of giving reasons and secondly because your feelings are not wholly private: others can help you determine what they amount to and what your central goals or purposes are. This is what we might expect, since it is familiar that we discover our identity, our central goals and purposes, through interaction with other people. It is worth adding that the open dialectic essential to freedom has implications for the way societies and institutions are run. Clearly it cannot flourish under authoritarianism, where some people claim the right to stand above the dialogue in virtue of their place in a hierarchy.

Two principal objections to the account I have given in this chapter need to be considered. The first can be expressed in Isaiah Berlin's often-quoted words (1969, p. 125): 'Everything is what it is: liberty is liberty, not equality or fairness or justice or culture, or human happiness or a quiet conscience' – or, it might be said, the discovery of identity or self-realization that I have described in what must fall on the positive side of the dividing line between the two different kinds of freedom. But perhaps Berlin's insistence that 'everything is what it is' is too quick and sweeping a way of settling the issue in favour of the negative view. If wants, feelings and purposes are as I have sketched, so that there can be internal motivational obstacles to a person doing what is most important to him and he must achieve a degree of self-understanding to be truly free, then it appears we have to abandon the negative view of freedom for *some* version of a positive one (cf. Taylor, 1979, esp. pp. 192–3).

The second objection is that education as a reflective enterprise, involving the discovery of one's identity, sounds narcissistic, a matter of examining one's navel. I do not think this is so. When you throw yourself wholeheartedly into any activity, whether it is

118

bird-watching, learning French or repairing a motor bike, to keep an eye on your progress in the activity is, since it is one which you identify as important to you, to be keeping an eye on yourself. Benn (1976) describes the dedicated potter:

> Recognising his pots as his *own* handiwork, his own responsibility, his appraisal is inevitably practical, associated with resolutions, hopes and projects for his future performance, over which he has a kind of control such as he has over the work of no one else. The very dissatisfaction he experiences in spotting imperfections and mistakes can motivate him to try harder and do better because they are ways of being dissatisfied with himself as the responsible creative agent.

We discover who we are, that is to say, what ends and purposes are significant to us, through the quality of our engagement with the world outside us. It is not that there are certain predetermined activities which are necessary to each and every human being (the constituent elements of rationality, on some positive views), nor that any activities at all will do so long as we want or choose them (a recognizable corollary of the negative view): it is how deeply, richly, absorbedly, reflectively we do the things we do that matters if we are to build through them a securer sense of who we really are.

Further Reading

Many of the issues I have discussed are treated in general introductions to the philosophy of education. Of these Louis Arnaud Reid's *Philosophy and Education* is one of the best. R. S. Peters's *Ethics and Education* was a standard text for many years and demands respect even if it may not command agreement.

Jonathan Glover's *Responsibility* includes discussion of determinism, blame and punishment. Chapter 9, 'Morality and evasion', is particularly worth reading. It contains, amongst other things, a powerful argument for making the techniques of philosophical criticism a central part of education.

Mary Midgley's *Beast and Man* contains discussion of human nature, freedom and culture. It is lively and highly readable: I cannot recommend it too strongly.

J. W. Docking's *Control and Discipline in Schools* is a comprehensive survey of this subject. It is a good guide to the literature, especially to empirical studies. Teacher–pupil relationships have received little explicit treatment from philosophers, who have tended to write of personal relationships in general. *Respect for Persons*, by R. S. Downie and Elizabeth Telfer, is somewhat Kantian in tone while *Understanding Persons*, by Frances Berenson, does justice to the place of feelings and emotions in personal relationships. Alasdair MacIntyre has some illuminating things to say about what he calls 'managerial attitudes' in *After Virtue*. The whole book is an excellent analysis of moral philosophy in its historical context. There are intriguing suggestions about attention and receptivity in Simone Weil's *Waiting on God*. Iris Murdoch brings out the importance of attention in *The Sovereignty of Good* as well as in her novels: the reader might start with *The Nice and the Good*.

The epistemological aspects of authority, that is the relations between authority and knowledge, are well treated by Kenneth Strike in *Liberty and Learning*. I disagree on numerous points with G. H. Bantock's thesis in *Freedom and Authority in Education*: all the more reason for the reader to study it. It is vigorous and challenging.

Anyone who hopes to understand the difficult philosophical question of punishment ought to read the two books by H. L. A. Hart that I have referred to. *Law, Liberty and Morality* is short and easy to read. *Punishment and Responsibility* contains two particularly important chapers, 'Prolegomenon to the principles of punishment' and 'Punishment and the elimination of responsibility'. Ted Honderich's *Punishment: The Supposed Justifications* is comprehensive but rather heavy going. P. S. Wilson's *Interest and Discipline in Education* deserves to be read carefully, including the first two chapters, on 'Needs' and 'Interests'.

The literature on freedom is enormous. A good place to start might be 'Enquiries for liberators', Chapter 3 of Janet Radcliffe Richards's *The Sceptical Feminist*. This is direct and forceful, although the writer is not always clear whether a liberator is concerned simply to *increase* options or rather to make available the ones that are *important*. John Stuart Mill's *On Liberty* is a classic, the place from which much of the debate about freedom starts. Aspects of Mill's book are discussed in *Of Liberty*, edited by A. Phillips Griffiths. This contains three essays of particular interest here: D. D. Raphael's 'Liberty and authority', Peter Gardner's 'Liberty and compulsory education' and David E. Cooper's 'The free man'. Isaiah Berlin's paper 'Two concepts of liberty' in his *Four Essays on Liberty* is an invaluable guide to some of the different conceptions of freedom that philosophers and others have entertained. *Philosophers Discuss Education*, edited by S. C. Brown, has sections on 'Autonomy as an educational ideal' and 'Academic freedom', the latter a subject I regret I have not had space to discuss myself.

I am conscious of having been perhaps too dismissive of the Kantian tradition in ethics. In recent writings it can be found at its best (and most influential) in R. M. Hare's *Freedom and Reason*. Kant's own moral philosophy is rather less one-dimensional than some of the work it has inspired. Anyone taking a serious interest in moral philosophy must read Kant's *Groundwork of the Metaphysic of Morals*, most conveniently in H. J. Paton's edition published as *The Moral Law*. A different ethical tradition is well represented by L. A. Blum's *Friendship, Altruism and Morality*.

I have been influenced by two books deeply critical of ideas which would usually be considered essentially Kantian: Michael Sandel's *Liberalism and the Limits of Justice* and Bernard Williams's collection of papers, *Moral Luck*. Neither book is elementary, but they are stimulating examples of work currently being done at what might be called the frontiers of the subject, and they hold important implications for education.

Bibliography

Aristotle (1969), *Nicomachean Ethics*, trans. D. Ross (London: Oxford University Press).

Ashton, F. (1982), 'Teacher education: a critical view of skills training', *British Journal of In-Service Education*, vol. 8, no. 3, pp. 160–7.

Bantock, G. H. (1952), *Freedom and Authority in Education* (London: Faber).

Barrow, R. (1976), *Common Sense and the Curriculum* (London: Allen & Unwin).

Beck, L. W. (1975), *The Actor and the Spectator* (London: Yale University Press).

Benn, S. I. (1976), 'Freedom, autonomy and the concept of a person', *Proceedings of the Aristotelian Society*, vol. LXXVI, 1975–6, pp. 109–30.

Benson, A. C. (1902), *The Schoolmaster* (London: John Murray).

Benson, J. (1983), 'Who is the autonomous man?' *Philosophy*, vol. 58, pp. 5–17.

Berenson, F. M. (1981), *Understanding Persons* (Brighton: Harvester).

Berg, L. (1977), *Reading and Loving* (London: Routledge & Kegan Paul).

Berlin, I. (1969), *Four Essays on Liberty* (London: Oxford University Press).

Blake, W. (1970), *Songs of Innocence and of Experience* (London: Oxford University Press).

Blum, L. A. (1980), *Friendship, Altruism and Morality* (London: Routledge & Kegan Paul).

Botros, S. (1983), 'Acceptance and morality', *Philosophy*, vol. 58, pp. 433–53.

Bradbury, M. (1975), *The History Man* (London: Secker & Warburg).

Brown, S. C. (ed.) (1975), *Philosophers Discuss Education* (London: Macmillan).

Bruner, J. S. (1960), *The Process of Education* (Cambridge, Mass.: Harvard University Press).

Carroll, J. (1979), 'Authority and the teacher', *Journal of Philosophy of Education*, vol. 13, pp. 133–40.

Corrigan, P. (1979), *Schooling the Smash Street Kids* (London: Macmillan).

Davies, B. (1979), *In Whose Interests?* (Leicester: National Youth Bureau).

Dearden, R. F. (1972), 'Autonomy and education', in R. F. Dearden, P. H. Hirst, and R. S. Peters (eds), *Education and The Development of Reason*, vol. 3, *Education and Reason* (London: Routledge & Kegan Paul), pp. 448–65.

Docking, J. W. (1980), *Control and Discipline in Schools* (London: Harper & Row).

122

Donaldson, M. (1978), *Children's Minds* (London: Fontana).

Dostoyevsky, F. (1982), *Crime and Punishment*, trans. D. Magarshack (Harmondsworth: Penguin).

Downie, R. S. and Telfer, E. (1971), *Respect for Persons* (London: Allen & Unwin).

Dworkin, R. (1977), *Taking Rights Seriously* (London: Duckworth).

Elliott, R. K. (1975), 'Education and human being I', in S. C. Brown (ed.), *Philosophers Discuss Education* (London: Macmillan), pp. 45–72.

FECRDU (Further Education Curriculum Review and Development Unit) (1980), *Developing Social and Life Skills* (London: HMSO).

FECRDU (1982), *Basic Skills* (London: HMSO).

Francis, P. (1975), *Beyond Control?* (London: Allen & Unwin).

Fromm, E. (1961), *The Art of Loving* (London: Allen & Unwin).

Glover, J. (1970), *Responsibility* (London: Routledge & Kegan Paul).

Griffiths, A. P. (ed.) (1983), *Of Liberty* (Cambridge: Cambridge University Press).

Gutman, A. (1980), 'Children, paternalism and education: a liberal argument', *Philosophy and Public Affairs*, vol. 9, no. 4, pp. 338–58.

Hannam, C., Smyth, P. and Stephenson, N. (1977), *Young Teachers and Reluctant Learners* (Harmondsworth: Penguin).

Hare, R. M. (1963), *Freedom and Reason* (Oxford: Clarendon).

Harris, J. (1982), The political status of children', in K. Graham, (ed.), *Contemporary Political Philosophy* (Cambridge: Cambridge University Press), pp. 35–55.

Hart, H. L. A. (1968), *Punishment and Responsibility* (Oxford: Clarendon).

Hart, H. L. A. (1969), *Law, Liberty and Morality* (London: Oxford University Press).

Haydon, G. (1978), 'On being responsible', *Philosophical Quarterly*, vol. 28, pp. 46–57.

Hirst, P. H. (1965), 'Liberal education and the nature of knowledge', in R. D. Archambault (ed.), *Philosophical Analysis and Education* (London: Routledge & Kegan Paul), pp. 113–38.

HMI (Her Majesty's Inspectorate) (1977), *Curriculum 11–16* (London: HMSO).

Hoggart, R. (1970), *Speaking to Each Other* (London: Chatto & Windus).

Holland, R. F. (1980), *Against Empiricism* (Oxford: Blackwell).

Holt, J. (1969), *How Children Fail* (Harmondsworth: Penguin).

Honderich, T. (1969), *Punishment: The Supposed Justifications* (London: Hutchinson).

Hughes, M. and Donaldson, M. (1979), 'The use of hiding games for studying coordination of viewpoints', *Educational Review*, vol. 31, pp. 133–40, repr. in M. Donaldson, R. Grieve and C. Pratt (eds), *Early Childhood Development and Education* (Oxford: Blackwell, 1983), pp. 245–53.

Hume, D. (1975), *Enquiries Concerning Human Understanding and Concerning the Principles of Morals*, ed. L. A. Selby-Bigge (Oxford: Clarendon).

Ibsen, H. (1965), *A Doll's House*, trans. P. Watts (Harmondsworth: Penguin).

123

Jonathan, R. (1982), 'The manpower service model of education', *Cambridge Journal of Education*, vol. 13, no. 2, pp. 3–10.

Kant, I. (1887), *The Philosophy of Law*, trans. W. Hastie (Edinburgh: T. & T. Clark).

Kant, I. (1976), *Groundwork of the Metaphysic of Morals*, trans. H. J. Paton as *The Moral Law* (London: Hutchinson).

Kerry, T. (1981), *Teaching Bright Pupils* (London: Macmillan).

Kerry, T. (1982), *Effective Questioning* (London: Macmillan).

Kounin, J. S. (1970), *Discipline and Group Management in Classrooms* (New York: Holt, Rinehart & Winston).

Langford, G. (1968), *Philosophy and Education* (London: Macmillan).

McGarrigle, J., Grieve, R. and Hughes, M. (1978), 'Interpreting inclusion: a contribution to the study of the child's cognitive and linguistic development', *Journal of Experiment Psychology*, vol. 25, pp. 1528–50, repr. in M. Donaldson, R. Grieve and C. Pratt (eds), *Early Childhood Development and Education* (Oxford: Blackwell, 1983), pp. 170–84.

MacIntyre, A. (1981), *After Virtue* (London: Duckworth).

Marland, M. (1980), *The Craft of the Classroom* (London: Heinemann).

Midgley, M. (1972), 'Is "moral" a dirty word?', *Philosophy*, vol. 47, pp. 206–28.

Midgley, M. (1980), *Beast and Man* (London: Methuen).

Mill, J. S. (1983), *On Liberty* (Harmondsworth: Penguin).

Murdoch, I. (1968), *The Nice and the Good* (London: Chatto & Windus).

Murdoch, I. (1970), *The Sovereignty of Good* (London: Routledge & Kegan Paul).

Orwell, G. (1970), *Nineteen Eighty-Four* (Harmondsworth: Penguin).

Peters, R. S. (1966), *Ethics and Education* (London: Allen & Unwin).

Peters, R. S. (1973), 'Freedom and the development of the free man', in J. F. Doyle (ed.), *Educational Judgements* (London: Routledge & Kegan Paul), pp. 119–42.

Plato (1968), *The Republic*, trans. D. Lee (Harmondsworth: Penguin).

Pring, R. (1976), *Knowledge and Schooling* (London: Open Books).

Rawls, J. (1972), *A Theory of Justice* (London: Oxford University Press).

Reid, L. A. (1965), *Philosophy and Education* (London: Heinemann).

Richards, J. R. (1982), *The Sceptical Feminist* (Harmondsworth: Penguin).

Rieff, P. (1973), *Fellow Teachers* (New York: Harper & Row).

Sandel, M. (1982), *Liberalism and the Limits of Justice* (Cambridge: Cambridge University Press).

Shweder, R. A., Turiel, E. and Much, N. C. (1981), 'The moral intuitions of the child', in J. H. Flavell and L. Ross (eds), *Social Cognitive Development* (Cambridge: Cambridge University Press), pp. 288–305.

Smith, F. (1971), *Understanding Reading* (New York: Holt, Rinehart & Winston).

Straughan, R. (1982a), *I Ought to, but . . .* (Windsor: NFER/Nelson).

Straughan, R. (1982b), 'What's the point of rules?', *Journal of Philosophy of Education*, vol. 16, no. 1, pp. 63–8.

Strike, K. (1982), *Liberty and Learning* (Oxford: Martin Robertson).

Taylor, C. (1979), 'What's wrong with negative liberty', in A. Ryan (ed.), *The Idea of Freedom* (London: Oxford University Press), pp. 175–93.

Watt, A. J. (1974), 'Forms of knowledge and norms of rationality', *Educational Philosophy and Theory*, vol. 6, pp. 1–11.

Weil, S. (1959), *Waiting on God*, trans. E. Craufurd (London: Fontana).

Wells, R. (1983), *Timothy Goes to School* (Harmondsworth: Penguin).

Weston, D. R. and Turiel, E. (1980), 'Act-rule relations: children's concepts of social rules', *Developmental Psychology*, vol. 16, pp. 417–24, repr. in M. Donaldson, R. Grieve and C. Pratt (eds), *Early Childhood Development and Education* (Oxford: Blackwell, 1983), pp. 54–65.

White, J. P. (1973), *Towards a Compulsory Curriculum* (London: Routledge & Kegan Paul).

White, P. (1983), *Beyond Domination* (London: Routledge & Kegan Paul).

Williams, B. (1981), *Moral Luck* (Cambridge: Cambridge University Press).

Wilson, J. (1977), *Philosophy and Practical Education* (London: Routledge & Kegan Paul).

Wilson, J. (1983), 'The purpose of retribution', *Philosophy*, vol. 58, pp. 521–7.

Wilson, P. S. (1971), *Interest and Discipline in Education* (London: Routledge & Kegan Paul).

Wilson, P. S. (1974), 'Perspectives on punishment', *Proceedings of the Philosophy of Education Society of Great Britain*, vol. 8, no. 1, pp. 103–34.

Winch, P. (1967), 'Authority', in A. Quinton (ed.), *Political Philosophy* (London: Oxford University Press), pp. 97–111.

Wragg, E. C. (1981), *Class Management and Control*) London: Macmillan).

Wragg, E. C. (1984), *Classroom Teaching Skills* (London: Croom Helm).

Index